# BETTE DAVIS

Grace Carter

For more information about New Word City, visit our Web site at
**www.newwordcity.com**

# INTRODUCTION

## "SHE DID IT THE HARD WAY."

In the course of a career tssfhat spanned six decades (from 1931 to 1989), more than 100 films, two Academy Awards, and ten Oscar nominations, Bette Davis became one of the greatest screen icons of all time. But her off-screen life was filled with drama and heartache. Even the title of her autobiography reflected the pain of her tumultuous existence.

It was called *The Lonely Life.*

Little came easily to Bette. Despite her success, she had to fight for first-rate roles and the directors that went along with them. She also struggled with addictions - alcohol and cigarettes, in particular. Married four times, she lived, for a while, under a cloud of suspicion after the only husband she didn't divorce died following a freak accident. She had three children, but even they brought her pain and controversy. Her eldest, B.D. Hyman, wrote a scathing, tell-all book in 1985, leaving permanent scars on Bette and her family; her second child, Margot, suffered a brain injury and had to live in an institution; her third, Michael, was the subject of a prolonged custody battle between Bette and her last husband, the actor Gary Merrill.

Despite such tribulations - and the fact that most of the films she appeared in bombed at the box office - Bette Davis managed to become, in the words of *New York Times* critic Terrence Rafferty, nothing less than "the greatest actress of the American cinema." During the 1930s and 1940s, when she was in her prime, she created a series of unforgettable characters - including the *femme fatale* Mildred Rogers in *Of Human Bondage* and the repressed spinster Charlotte Vale in *Now, Voyager* - and won Oscars for both *Dangerous* (1935) and *Jezebel* (1938). In 1950, she gave what many consider her finest performance, as the aging Broadway star Margo Channing in the classic *All About Eve*. Said Rafferty: "She was as electrifying as Marlon Brando in the fifties: volatile, sexy, challenging, fearlessly inventive. She looked moviegoers straight in the eye and dared them to look away."

What made Bette stand out was her fierce desire

to play characters who behaved badly - even sadistically or brutally - at a time when most actresses were preoccupied with their appearance. "The cornerstone of my career in films was the power for action with which all women identified," Bette said once. "When I portrayed evil on the screen, the women of the world were purged of suppressed violence and sheer boredom."

Clearly, Bette was not a conventional star. She wasn't a great beauty like Marlene Dietrich, Greta Garbo, or Jean Harlow. (Bette had "a fat little Dutch girl's face and a neck that's too long," said her first makeup man.) But she had something far more important: a restless, incandescent energy that made her mesmerizing on the big screen. As the British novelist and critic E. Arnot Robertson said, "She gives the curious feeling of being charged with power which can find no ordinary outlet."

And then there were those eyes. For some, they were freakish - "bug eyes declaring a strangeness that beguiled and fascinated," said film historian Elaine Lennon. To others, they were sexy and bewitching, immortalized in the Kim Carnes song, *Bette Davis Eyes*, which became a hit in 1981 and introduced Davis to a new generation of fans.

Her long career showed that transcendent acting and a distinctive look mattered far more, in the end, than the ephemeral allure of conventional beauty. In her fifties, Bette proved her staying power with roles in the popular horror films *What Ever Happened to Baby Jane?* (1962) and *Hush . . . Hush, Sweet Charlotte* (1964). But even in such movies, later regarded as camp classics, her artistry shows through. Bette did not disappear into a role; rather, her characters always reflected the larger-than-life personality of the actress who created them. That included her many quirks, such as strutting forcefully into a scene, clenching her fists, and making masterful use of those mysterious, darting eyes. "Davis was a vulgar, bullying actress who made mannerism a virtue by showing us how it expresses the emanation of the self," wrote Peter McNally in his book, *Bette Davis: The Performances That Made Her Great.*

Her later horror films helped turn Bette into an icon, in among other things, America's gay subculture. But in the eyes of some critics, such fame did not help her reputation as a serious artist. "Was she just a camp figurehead because her brittle, melodramatic style of acting hadn't aged well?" asked the journalist Jim Emerson. "Or was it that she was 'Larger Than Life,' a tough broad who had survived? Probably some of both."

As Bette grew older, that sense of survival became her hallmark. In her seventies, she forged ahead and continued to make movies and television shows despite health setbacks, including breast cancer and a stroke that left her partly paralyzed.

As she put it, in perhaps her most famous quote, "Old age ain't no place for sissies." She smoked a hundred cigarettes a day and died in 1989 at the age of eighty-one.

"She was a magnificently talented actress, but the emotional baggage she brought with her was awesome," said producer William Frye, writing in *Vanity Fair* magazine in 2010. Those personal issues – manifest in her constant, vicious battles with directors, studio chiefs, producers, co-stars, husbands, and children – were on full display in her two memoirs, the first published in 1962, the second in 1987. She also contributed to a 1974 book by Whitney Stine called *Mother Goddamn*, a name from one of her movies that Bette adopted for herself and encouraged her children to call her.

Among her adversaries in her legendary Hollywood feuds were a who's who of motion-picture history: Miriam Hopkins, Errol Flynn, and her arch-nemesis, Joan Crawford. Her affairs with prominent men were waged just as passionately; her romantic conquests included the eccentric tycoon Howard Hughes, songwriter Johnny Mercer, and her favorite director, William Wyler.

And yet, even to those she fought with and loved, Bette remained something of an enigma. "Her life was bold and punchy, full of contradictions," wrote the film critic Rex Reed. "Distant yet intimate, bitchy yet humane, controlled yet flamboyant, a firebrand longing for domesticity, she bristled with the kind of neurotic tension that is often mistaken for creative energy."

Near the end of her life, she became even more caustic, nearly a parody of herself. As her drinking increased, she tossed off nasty letters to friends and settled old scores. Through it all, though, she had few regrets. Reflection and self-doubt were never her style. "Being hysterical is like having an orgasm," she once said. "It's good for you."

How the baby girl born Ruth Elizabeth Davis in Lowell, Massachusetts, in April 1908 became the legendary Bette Davis is a fascinating tale rich with intrigue, passion, and surprising plot twists. Like any good story, it has plenty of conflict, much of it created by a protagonist who always delighted in a good fight. "I have been at war from the beginning," she wrote in her autobiography. "I rode into the field with sword gleaming and standard flying. I was going to conquer the world."

# 1

# "I HAPPENED BETWEEN A CLAP OF THUNDER AND A STREAK OF LIGHTNING."

Given what is now known about Bette Davis, it should come as no surprise that she emerged from a long line of strong-willed women. Her grandmother on her mother's side, Eugenia Favor, was "five feet of TNT," Bette once said. With little patience for idle hands and minds, Eugenia insisted that her four children – Paul, Ruth, Mildred, and Richard – take piano lessons, read Emerson, Wordsworth, and the Bible, and obey her commands without question.

Bette's mother, Ruthie, inherited Eugenia's energy and talent, though not her strictness. Growing up in Lowell at the turn of the century, she was more esthete than drill sergeant, a tomboy who insisted on being called "Fred," starred in high-school plays, and painted and sketched. By her teenage years, she was beautiful, graceful, and, in Bette's words, "filled with the joy of life."

That made her an odd match for Harlow Morrell Davis, the man she would marry. Ruthie and Harlow had known each other since childhood, since both families spent their summers vacationing in the resort town of Ocean Park, Maine. The son of a Baptist deacon in Augusta, Maine, Harlow grew up to be tall and gaunt, with a protruding forehead and glasses, and an almost comically serious disposition. At Bates College, he was Phi Beta Kappa, president of his class for all four years, and a champion debater.

Harlow had none of Eugenia's artistic inclinations, either. "He approached life as if it were a soluble problem in geometry," Bette said of her father.

Both sides of Bette's family were early American settlers. The Davis clan, originally from Wales, helped found the city of Haverhill, Massachusetts, in 1640; the French Favors helped settle New Rochelle, New York, in 1688. As Harlow pursued Ruthie, Eugenia was impressed by the young man's lineage – and family money – and urged her daughter to accept his marriage proposal. Ironically, Harlow's mother was the one who tried to talk Ruthie out of it. Though her son was brilliant, Mrs. Davis told her, he was a disagreeable young man. "He will make your life miserable, my dear," she said.

But the stubborn Eugenia got her way, as always, and the young couple took their vows on July 1, 1907. Harlow was twenty-two, his bride just twenty. At ceremony's end, Ruthie got a glimpse of what she was in for. As the happy guests tossed confetti and rice at the bride and groom, Harlow became enraged at the indignity of this tradition of being pelted with uncooked grain and colorful scraps of paper. He turned toward them and bellowed, "God damn you, I'll get you for this!"

When Ruthie got pregnant on their honeymoon, Harlow flew into a rage again. By then a student at Harvard Law School, he had not planned to start a family so soon. But fate had other plans. After they moved into Eugenia's home on Chester Street in Lowell, Ruth Elizabeth – they called her Betty – was born during a terrible thunderstorm on the night of April 5, 1908.

"I happened between a clap of thunder and a streak of lightning," Bette said later, with her usual dramatic flair. "It almost hit the house and destroyed a tree out front. As a child, I fancied that the Finger of God was directing the attention of the world to me."

The stress of parenthood widened the gulf between Harlow and Ruthie. He became irritated that she did not share his intellectual passions and was mystified by her enthusiasm for the baby. Bette later said she could not recall a single moment of affection between her parents. But she did recall the verbal abuse. "Father's wit was a knife," she said. "He sharpened it on mother."

When Harlow began his career as a patent attorney for the United Shoe Machinery Company of Boston, the family moved to the suburb of Winchester. There, Ruthie gave birth to another child, Barbara Harriet "Bobby," on October 25, 1909. The presence of another child did not have a mellowing effect on Harlow. As the girls grew up, they were not allowed to sit at the dining room table with the adults except on Sunday – and even then, they often ended up in tears when their father sent them away for some infraction, including not being witty enough. "Bobby spent every waking moment trying to please Daddy," Bette recalled later. "I somehow knew it would never work. I simply kept out of his way."

To compensate for her husband's coldness, Ruthie heaped love and attention upon her children. Thanks to her mother, Bette remembers plenty of happy moments from her early childhood: sunny afternoons on a swing in their yard and snowy days when she and Bobby would slide down a hill behind their house. Christmas was always fun, thanks to the odd fact that their father mysteriously changed from The Grinch to Santa Claus at that time of year. He decorated the tree and showered the girls with gifts; gaiety filled their home. Christmas, in fact, was the only time Bette remembered the whole family laughing together.

But the underlying psychological dynamics were complex and often tempestuous. Sensing that her mother was being extra kind to offset their father's remoteness, young Betty took full advantage, throwing tantrums to get what she wanted. She had a strange obsession with neatness and order – which continued into adulthood – and would explode in fury if anything was awry, even an unlaced shoe. One Sunday, as she was being dressed to visit Grandmother Favor, Bette began screaming bloody murder. Neither her worried mother nor her annoyed father could figure out what was wrong until Ruthie finally removed the girl's dress – which had a large wrinkle on the front – and put on a freshly ironed one. Immediately, Bette stopped crying and smiled, revealing her first tooth. Order was restored.

The combination of an overcompensating mother, a distant father, a sense of entitled destiny by the child – plus Bette's own hot temper - was the perfect formula to create a demanding, egocentric star. "I was always going to be somebody," she recalled. "I didn't know exactly what at first - perhaps the beautiful nurse in the Red Cross posters immaculately extending her hand of mercy to the world . . ."

Because of her strong-willed ways, Bette always seemed to be in the family spotlight, with her younger sister shunted aside. From the time Bobby was born, Bette saw her as a rival. Once, Bette removed her sister from her crib – which Bette felt belonged to her – and placed her face down on a couch (fortunately, the baby was quickly rescued by the nanny). Bette was, in effect, kicking Bobby off her property. Later, she cut off Bobby's hair, saying, "Now she isn't going to be pretty."

Bette's need to overshadow her sister was so great, in fact, that her memoirs devote little space to describing what Bobby was like or how they interacted - a typically vague line: "We are different as night and day." Bette did make it clear, however, that she was the star of the family and Bobby was playing a supporting role.

As conflicted as her childhood was, Bette still had a relatively stable place to call home for the first seven years of her life. All that changed when the Davis family began coming apart. Her ambitious father, regarded as one of the country's top patent attorneys, felt increasingly constrained by his wife and children, with whom he had little in common.

The moment her father abandoned the family became seared into Bette's memory. One night, they all went out to dinner at a fancy restaurant in Boston. It was a farewell, of sorts - but only temporary, she was assured. Mother was taking Betty and Bobby to Florida on vacation, and their father was sending them off. The occasion was supposed to be festive - a string orchestra was playing, and hot rolls were being served on a silver wagon. For dessert, there was lemon sherbet.

But Bette could not help noticing that her parents barely ate and did not look well. Then Harlow took his family to the railway station, kissed his wife and children, and stood on the platform as the train pulled away. When they got to Florida, Ruthie explained that their Daddy would not be living with them anymore. The message was clear: Their father did not want them. "Bobby cried her eyes out," Bette recalled, adding that she was more pragmatic. "I started planning our life without him."

After their trip to Florida, Ruthie and her girls lived briefly in Newton, Massachusetts. Determined to give her children a good education - and realizing that Harlow's alimony payments were not enough to pay for it - Bette's mother decided to take extreme measures. She moved to New York City, found a job as a governess for three little boys, and sent her daughters to a boarding school on a farm in the Berkshires of Western Massachusetts.

It was the beginning of a long and difficult period for the family as Ruthie struggled to support her children and provide the education and life experiences she felt they needed, even if it meant being separated from them for long stretches.

The girls' new school, Crestalban, had only thirteen

students who all lived together on a functioning farm with pigs, cows, horses, and chickens. In addition to the basics of reading, writing, and arithmetic, the kids were taught sewing, cooking, and house cleaning. Only French was spoken at lunch. They were outside eighteen hours a day, sleeping on a porch and sitting by a roaring fire at night doing their mending while a teacher read aloud to them. For the girls, it was a huge adjustment, but ultimately, Bette came to embrace the rigors of their rugged life. "I adored it," she said.

Crestalban was the girls' home for six years, until the fall of 1921, when Ruthie decided she could not be separated from them any longer. Bette was thirteen, Bobby almost twelve. Ruthie may also have been pushed to make the change by a horrible accident Bette suffered at school: She was dressed as Santa Clause when her beard and sleeves caught fire from a candle perched on the Christmas tree (the school had no electricity for lights). Her face was badly burned, and it took weeks of painful recovery before she was fully healed.

Ruthie, meanwhile, had decided to fulfill a longstanding dream by enrolling in Clarence White's School of Photography in New York City and eventually became a portrait photographer. She rented a one-bedroom apartment on 144th Street and Broadway and enrolled her children in the neighborhood public school, P.S. 186. Finally, the family was back together again.

Going from a Spartan country life to a big city was another difficult transition for the girls; they burst into tears when they stepped inside their tiny new apartment with its musty old furniture and what Bette described as "sleazy pink lace curtains" on the windows. But soon enough, they adjusted and came to love urban life - the Italian ice, roller skating on the sidewalks, and spying on neighbors through the windows.

During this time, Bette made a profound change in her identity, and it happened in a random, off-handed way. A close friend of their mother, Myrtis Genthner, was reading Balzac's *La Cousine Bette* and suggested that the teenage Betty change the spelling of her name to Bette - but still pronounce it "Betty" - for no other reason than "to set you apart, my dear."

Bette liked the idea. When her father received a letter from his daughter, signing her name "Bette," he replied by saying the change made him laugh, and he dismissed it as a passing fancy. That sealed the deal. "Just tell me I'm not going to do something," she said later. "I do it. My name forever after was spelled B-E-T-T-E."

Ruthie, meanwhile, kept the family moving as she tried to find the right combination of good schools, safe neighborhoods, and photography jobs.

In the fall of 1922, they moved to a boarding house in East Orange, New Jersey - for once because of Bobby. The previous summer, while at a camp in Fryeburg, Maine, Bobby had shown such talent playing piano that the teacher urged Ruthie to continue her lessons in New Jersey. Excited that her younger daughter was displaying some talent, Ruthie made the move. This upset Bette, of course. She hated living in a boarding house and, even more, was annoyed that Bobby was getting more attention than she was.

Partly to mollify Bette, Ruthie moved the family yet again - to Newton, Massachusetts, where Bette enrolled in the public high school. Also, Ruthie had developed a painful inflammation in her jaw and needed help with the kids from her sister Mildred, who lived in Newton.

Now a teenager, Bette was proving too difficult for her mother to handle. After consulting a doctor, Ruthie decided that her eldest daughter was "a high-spirited race horse and needed a free rein," as she put it, so from then on, there would be few rules or discipline. "She had little choice," Bette recalled. "The filly became a bucking bronco."

Later, Ruthie told Bette that she was afraid of her during those years. At the slightest provocation, the girl would give her mother a nasty glare, leaving Ruthie to giggle nervously. "I sensed my power over her and my irritation grew greater when she surrendered," Bette recalled. "There was no pleasing me. Her nervous chatter, meant to buck us up, insulted my intelligence and earned a smirk of contempt when I was in a mood. Poor Ruthie!"

At wit's end, Ruthie suggested that she and Bette exchange clothes and personalities for one night, just for fun. At dinner, Bette's mom did a spot-on impersonation - "sulking and glowering into her spinach ramekin and being generally obnoxious," Bette recalled. It was so uncanny, in fact, that Bette flipped out. "I'm *not* like that," she yelled, storming out of the room. "That's *not* me!" Deep down, she knew her mother was right, but the whole exercise did little to curb her impulsive misbehavior.

Her mother wasn't the only one Bette wanted to dominate. At age sixteen, she started to discover her power over the opposite sex. She began dating many boys at Newton High and then at the private Cushing Academy in Ashburnham, Massachusetts, after she transferred there in early 1926, her junior year.

She was amazed at how she could manipulate the boys with a smile or frown – but she did not let them get far in their amorous pursuits. She had deeply absorbed the Puritan values of her family, especially Grandmother Favor and Ruthie's brother Paul, an Episcopalian minister who intermittently tried to make up for the absence of a father figure in her life. Bette spurned the boys' advances so rigorously, in fact, that in the Cushing seniors' yearbook bequests to their lower classmen, they left Bette "two dozen handkerchiefs to blow her 'no's' with."

Bette was also beginning to see that she often rubbed people the wrong way. Despite being a good student and the president of her sorority, she only got one vote in her campaign for student-body president because, she realized, the other kids thought she was stuck-up. She wasn't, she insisted later, but she was quite sure of herself - a quality that turned many people off, especially coming from a girl.

One student who didn't mind her self-assurance in the least was her future husband, Harmon "Ham" Nelson. Since Ham was a senior and Bette a junior, they only overlapped for one year - but the attraction was immediate. Tall and lean with dark and curly hair, he was not a football player or enormously popular. He had a "funny nose," Bette said, but she was transfixed by his beautiful brown eyes and his musical ability. He played piano, took up trumpet, and their first sparks occurred when he suggested they collaborate on a song for a school performance. She agreed, singing "Gee, I'm Mighty Blue for You" while he accompanied her on the piano.

"What a prophetic title," Bette said later. "Many times in the years since our divorce, I will find myself singing this song which takes me back to those early years with Ham. Such nostalgia - so in love - so in love in a way one can never be again."

That summer, Bette began to realize she had talent as a stage performer. But as a dancer, not an actress. Her mother had decided the family would spend their school vacation in Peterborough, New Hampshire, where she hoped to find work photographing events at Mariarden, a local school for dance and theater. It was all a big gamble - typical behavior for Ruthie, who always had some crazy dream or adventurous scheme to follow and didn't hesitate to drag her two daughters along for the ride.

Not only did Ruthie find work shooting school performances, but Mariarden's prominent dance instructor, named Roshanara, was so impressed by Bette's ability that she offered her free tuition to study there. As part of the deal, the teacher also agreed to hire her sister Bobby as a rehearsal pianist for $5 a week.

Bette danced eight hours a day for the next eight weeks and loved every moment. From Roshanara, she learned how to express her emotions and personality in movement, in ways that words never could – skills she would later use in her films to great effect. That summer, she appeared as a dancing fairy in *Midsummer Night's Dream*. Later, the director of the play, the well-regarded British stage and film actor Frank Conroy approached

Ruthie. "I seldom tell a mother what I am going to tell you," he said. "You must see to it your daughter goes on the stage. She belongs there. She has something which comes across the footlights."

Bette was not sure that performing on stage was her calling, however. And she had other things on her mind. Back at Cushing in the fall, she missed Ham, who was now attending Massachusetts Agriculture College. Voted the prettiest girl in the senior class, she played the lead in the senior play, but the experience was so forgettable that later she could even forget the name of the show.

When it came time to graduate, Ruthie had to take all the senior class pictures to earn enough money to pay Bette's tuition – including developing the negatives and printing each one by hand. "As long as I live, my greatest incentive to become a success in the world was the sight of my mother sitting in the assembly hall at my graduation," Bette said later.

As she accepted her diploma, Bette looked out at the crowd and spotted Ruthie: "She had developer poisoning very apparent on her face - she weighed about ninety pounds - as a result of finishing all the orders for the graduating class in time, a last-year's dress and hat, and a tired but proud smile on her face. A braver, more exhausted mother was not there that day. I wanted to cry. I remember thinking as I looked down at her that I must repay her for all these years of blood, sweat, and no tears."

After spending the summer of 1927 in Ogunquit, Maine – where Bette betrayed Ham by having a fling with a Yale boy named Fritz Hall – the family returned to Newton so Bobby could finish high school. Ever since Frank Conroy told Ruthie that her daughter belonged on stage, Bette had thought more and more about becoming an actress, but it seemed an impossible path. Her mother simply didn't have the money to send her to New York to study theater. So maybe acting wasn't her destiny after all. Whatever her future path, she said later, she was sure it would be something very important: "Suburbia, husband, children, bridge clubs would never be for me."

Feeling lost, Bette moped around the house, a recent high-school graduate working occasionally as a freelance typist to earn money. Her life was going nowhere. Even when Ham returned to visit at Christmas – by then she had lost interest in Fritz Hall – their dreams of a future together seemed more distant than ever.

Then Henrik Ibsen changed her life. Ruthie took her girls to the Jewett Playhouse in Boston to see Ibsen's *The Wild Duck*. It was Bette's first contact with serious theater. In Act Two, Gina Ekdal is sewing while her fourteen-year-old daughter Hedvig sits on a sofa reading.

"Hedvig!" Gina says.

The child does not hear; she is too engrossed in her book.

"Hedvig!"

When the girl finally looks up, Bette's heart nearly stopped. "She looked just like me," she recalled later.

"Hedvig dear, you mustn't sit reading any longer now."

"Oh mother, mayn't I read a little more? Just a little bit?"

"No, no, you must put away your book now. Father doesn't like it . . ."

As she sat in the theater, Bette recalled, "I was watching myself." The actress, Peg Entwistle, had completely disappeared into the part of Hedvig. So had Bette. "There wasn't an emotion I didn't anticipate and share with her," she said. "In some incredible fusion, Entwistle, Hedvig and I were now one."

When Hedvig, "the little wild duck" of the play's title, shot herself in the breast, Bette felt that she was dying, too. "I had no pulse whatsoever as Hedvig was carried from the stage in a little casket," she said later. "It seemed as though everything in my life fell into place and I was in focus for the first time. There had been a glimmer here and there; but this was the vision."

At eighteen, Bette suddenly knew for sure what she wanted to do with her life. "Mr. Conroy had known before I did," she recalled. "I knew now that more than anything - despite anything - I was going to become an actress."

"Mother!" Bette cried. "Someday I will play Hedvig."

# 2

# "I THOUGHT THE RAIN HAD CAUSED THE ROOF TO CAVE IN. IT WAS THE AUDIENCE. IT WAS APPLAUSE."

Ever since her parents divorced, Bette did not see much of her father. But he did provide her with a great deal of inspiration – to do exactly the opposite of whatever he wanted. So when Ruthie told Harlow their daughter had her heart set on becoming an actress, he provided plenty of extra motivation by saying, "Let her become a secretary! She'll earn money quicker. Bette could never be a successful actress."

Bette's grandmother Eugenia, however, was extremely supportive: "Believe in something," she said. "Work for it. It will be yours!"

The moment Bette had her epiphany while watching her first Ibsen play, Ruthie got to work, looking for any opportunity to help her daughter achieve her dream. In the fall of 1927, she drove Bette, now nineteen, to New York for an interview with the Broadway star Eva Le Gallienne, who ran a highly regarded theater school on Fourteenth Street. Confident and burning with desire, Bette was sure she would be accepted.

But the interview did not go smoothly. Bette became flustered when Le Gallienne asked strange questions like, "Why should acting students study the movements of animals?" She wondered what that had to do with acting. As the famous actress probed and prodded her, Bette felt uncomfortable, defensive, even stupid. She thrived on approval; that day, she was getting none.

The worst moment came when Le Gallienne asked her to read the part of a sixty-five-year-old Dutch woman. Bette tried to politely decline, knowing it would be a stretch. "That is why I want to come to your school, to learn how to play a part like this," she blurted out. Silence. Bette read the part with gritted teeth. The interview was over.

An agonizing week later, the letter from Le Gallienne came. It said that Bette was not serious enough in her approach to acting and would not be admitted. Heartbroken and angry, Bette was certain that her dreams of acting stardom were over and she would be stuck in Newton, Massachusetts for the rest of her life.

But Ruthie was not ready to give up. She decided to move with Bette to Norwalk, Connecticut to bring them closer to the theater scene of New York.

Soon, Ruthie found a job doing retouching work for a local photographer. Bobby, who had one year left at Newton High, moved in with Ruthie's sister Mildred and her husband Myron. Once again, Ruthie had placed Bette's needs over Bobby's, reinforcing the younger sister's feelings of inferiority and abandonment. "We hated leaving Bobby," Bette recalled later. "Poor Ruthie was always torn when feeling the necessity of separating any of the three of us."

Despite the change of location, Bette was still sad that her life was going nowhere – except when she slipped away to visit her old beau Fritz Hall in nearby New Haven. Ever fickle, she had once again forgotten all about Ham. Since she and Ruthie lived in a small room in a rooming house, she spent most of her days wandering around Norwalk, occasionally stopping by the studio where her mother worked. She could see Ruthie in the window, hunched over photo negatives for hours at a time as she did her painstaking retouching work – "another image of Ruthie's gallantry I never forgot," Bette said later.

One morning, Ruthie told her daughter they were taking the train to New York without explaining why; she loved surprising her daughter. When they arrived, Bette was delighted to discover that Ruthie had scheduled a meeting with Hugh Anderson, the manager of the John Murray Anderson School for the Dramatic Arts. While Bette waited outside Anderson's office, Ruthie told him, "My daughter Bette wants to be an actress. I haven't the money for her tuition but will assure you, you will eventually have it. Will you accept her as a student?"

Anderson, taken aback but impressed by Ruthie's boldness, somehow found himself saying yes. "A miracle happened on 58th Street that day," Bette recalled later. "Ruthie found a way to open the door so I could pursue my dream."

The next day, Ruthie quit her job and they moved to New York. After enrolling, Bette was assigned a room in a brownstone boardinghouse on East Fifty-Eighth Street next door to the school, sharing her space with another student. Once she was settled, Ruthie found a job as a housemother at St. Mary's School in Burlington, New Jersey, some eighty miles away.

The John Murray Anderson School, during the 1927-28 term, gave Bette just what she needed - a solid foundation in the fundamentals of acting. The students performed in a play once a week and spent the rest of the time memorizing lines, rehearsing, and studying various aspects of theater. In a matter of months, Bette transformed her voice - a high, tiny squeak when she started - into a powerful instrument that could be heard in the back of the theater. She also worked diligently to get rid of her thick Boston accent so that she no longer elicited giggles when she spoke.

Her acting teacher, George Currie, delivered a daily diatribe to his class about how difficult life in show business can be - full of sweat, jealousy, competition, disillusionment, and insecurity. Most of the students became so discouraged by these rants that by the end of the semester, just twelve of the original seventy students remained. Only the real artists stayed, those who were strong enough to take it.

"Everything he said was true," Bette said later. "Any artist who doesn't know that the greatest reward is his own satisfaction in work should choose an easier way of life."

One of her favorite teachers was Martha Graham, then in her thirties and on the cusp of the achievements that would make her a legend in the dance world. "To act is to dance!" she told the students. From Graham, Bette learned a physical syntax with which to express herself and how to convey a gamut of emotions – anguish, joy, hatred, ecstasy, compassion – through disciplined body movements. (Complimented later about her ability to convey complex meaning non-verbally, Bette said: "Every time I climbed a flight of stairs in films - and I spent half my life on them - it was Graham, step by step.")

But while at the Anderson school, Bette received a marriage proposal from Fritz Hall that offered her a stark choice: Continue to chase her acting dream or quit to become a housewife. Bette wore his engagement ring for three days while he begged her to leave school. Hall planned to go into his father's business after college and needed a wife and a hostess. To him, acting was a lark a young woman might pursue before marriage but not the proper sort of activity for the future Mrs. Hall.

Bette never responded well to ultimatums, nor was she receptive to this one. She was unmoved by the news clippings Hall sent about Katherine Willson, an actress who announced that she was giving up her promising theatrical career to get married, saying, "A woman's place is in the home." Marrying Hall would mean her money worries would be over, Bette knew, but she returned the ring - and resumed exchanging letters with Ham.

By the end of her first year, Bette had won the lead role in *The Famous Mrs. Fair,* a Broadway play that had been made into a 1923 silent film. The stakes were high. She would be graded on her performance and observed by visitors from the theater world, students, and parents. A poor showing could endanger the full year's scholarship she had applied for.

Two days before the show, Bette contracted laryngitis. She tried every cold remedy possible, but nothing worked. She went on stage, as scheduled, and by Act III, her voice began to give way. But somehow, she held on, using her raspy voice to great dramatic effect, and turning in a bravura performance. Not only did she win the scholarship, but a week later, the director, James Light, of the prestigious Provincetown Playhouse in Greenwich Village, offered her a role in a play later that spring. Bette was ecstatic - her first professional job!

But there was a catch: Light said she would have to quit school to devote herself fully to the part. Confused, Bette went to Hugh Anderson for advice, and was surprised but grateful when he advised her to take advantage of this golden opportunity.

A few weeks later, she quit and excitedly began preparing for rehearsals. But soon afterward, Light informed her that the play was being postponed until the fall. She never found out why, but it didn't matter - suddenly, Bette was out of school and out of work.

At a loss, she decided to write to Frank Conroy, the actor who had been so encouraging during her stint at the Mariarden school in New Hampshire. Conroy sent her a letter of introduction to director George Cukor, who was casting a production of the crime drama *Broadway* at a theater in Rochester, New York.

Cukor, who would go on to become one of

Hollywood's most acclaimed directors, did not seem terribly impressed by Bette when they met for an interview. But he gave her a small part as a chorus girl for one week. It was obvious that he was doing it as a favor to Conroy, but Bette didn't care - it was a paying gig, her first ever.

Ruthie could not go with her to Rochester - she had to finish out the school year at St. Mary's - but she came to the train station in New York to say goodbye. "Learn the part of Pearl," Ruthie said as the train pulled away. "The actress playing the part is going to have an accident."

"Oh, Mother!" Bette said laughing. "You and your hunches." But she knew Ruthie's hunches were nothing to sneer at. Her mother read tea leaves with unerring accuracy. And one night just over a year earlier, Bette had gone on her first unchaperoned date in Ogunquit, Maine, when her mother had a premonition that something was wrong. She sent a young man to rush to the dance she was attending and take her home immediately. When he arrived, Bette objected, but he insisted and they finally left the party. The next morning, the boy who had brought her to the dance appeared to give Ruthie a hug. "Thank God, you sent for Bette last night," he said. "One of my friends drove the car home - and completely smashed it up. Bette would most likely have been killed."

So Bette decided to take her mother's latest hunch

seriously and started studying the role of Pearl on the train, just in case. Soon, she had the whole part memorized. The play opened successfully on a Monday but during the Wednesday matinee, Rose Lerner, who played Pearl, twisted her ankle badly during a choreographed moment when she had to fall down a flight of stairs. She limped through that performance and used a cane that night.

The following morning, Bette arrived early at the theater, hoping for her chance. When Cukor arrived, he yelled to his stage manager, "Get that dame who has the smallest part over here right away." Unruffled that he didn't even know her name, Bette said, "I'm here, Mr. Cukor."

The director asked if she could learn the part by that evening. Bette said she already knew it. So Cukor asked her to fall down a flight of stairs which - thanks to Martha Graham's training - she executed perfectly. They rehearsed Pearl's scenes and Bette went on that night.

Bette performed flawlessly except when it came time for Pearl to shoot her lover. She was supposed to fire just two shots at the actor, Robert Strange. Then he would stagger off into the wings so he would not have to lie on stage pretending to be dead for the rest of the act. But Bette had always been afraid of guns, fireworks, or any kind of loud noises. She was in such a state of terror about using the weapon - and nervous in her first professional acting role -

that she shot Strange so many times he could not believably stumble offstage. So he was forced to lie there on stage, trying to hold his breath, until the curtain for the act finally came down.

After the show, Strange was polite but insistent. "Miss Davis, tomorrow night will you do me a favor - only fire two bullets, so I can get offstage?"

By Saturday night, Bette's contract was over, but Cukor was so impressed that he offered her the ingénue lead for the company's next season in the fall. "God bless Ruthie's gypsy ways!" she thought.

After going back to her old farm school of Crestalban for a few weeks to help stage its graduation play, Bette drove with Ruthie and Bobby - who had just graduated from high school - to Cape Cod, where the family would spend the summer of 1928. A job was waiting for Bette with a summer stock company, the Cape Playhouse.

At least she thought it was. An agent in New York had connected her with the theater's director, who was impressed by her drive and had hired her on the spot. But when she showed up at the Cape Playhouse, the owner, Raymond Moore, said the director was not authorized to hire actors; the best he could offer her was a job as an usher. Bette was angry at first, then relieved that she at least had a paying job.

After showing audience members to their seats, Bette memorized all the lines of the ingénue, hoping for another sprained ankle. There were no freak accidents this time, but when the company prepared to perform A. A. Milne's Mr. *Pirn Passes By*, an opportunity did arise.

Laura Hope Crewes, who starred in the play on Broadway to great success, would be reprising her role and also directing. But she was unhappy with the actress slated to play Dinah, an English girl. When Crewes demanded that Moore replace her with someone more suitable, he suggested Bette, impressed that she had so gracefully made the transition from rejected actress to diligent usher.

"Well, my dear, if you can play and sing the English ballad, 'I Passed by Your Window,' by ten o'clock Monday morning, the part of Dinah is yours," Crewes said.

As exciting as the offer was, it presented some problems. The ballad was not in the script and nobody in the company knew it. And it was already Saturday afternoon. Ruthie drove her girls quickly to Hyannis, the nearest town, but the proprietor of the only music store in town had never even heard of the song. Bette was despondent but Ruthie, as usual, was not about to give up. They checked all the local churches until finding an organist who, after three hours of digging, finally produced a copy of the ballad. Eureka! The kindly rector allowed Bette to use the church piano, so she practiced for the rest of the weekend.

On Monday morning, Bette played and sang the song for Crewes on the theater's Steinway. The part of Dinah was hers. During rehearsals, Bette had to learn to control a quirky habit she had developed of fluttering her arms about when she spoke. But when opening night arrived, she gave a solid performance and received a big ovation. Regular audience members who knew Bette as their usher were excited to see her transformation into an actress.

"I was good as Dinah and I knew it," Bette recalled later. "My ecstasy knew no bounds. I had been rewarded for being a good sport." Even better, Moore asked her to come back the following season as the company ingénue.

That Cape Cod summer was also notable for the crush Bette developed on one of the young actors, Henry Fonda. The future movie star never returned her affection, Bette said later, but he did come to dinner once at the cottage Ruthie had rented. Later, Bette said, "I have to admit I did not remain faithful to Hank forever, but that summer he was the most beautiful boy I had ever seen - besides being *such* a good actor."

As the summer came to a close, Bobby decided to move to Granville, Ohio to attend Denison University. She was tired of living under the shadow of her outgoing, successful sister, and wanted to establish her own identity. Much quieter than either her mother or sister, Bobby had become exhausted by the turmoil and drama that always seemed to follow the Davis family. "Love us she did," Bette said later. "'Wanted out' she did also."

Ruthie and her eldest, meanwhile, headed for Rochester, New York, so Bette could begin her job as the ingénue with George Cukor's stock company, now called the Temple Players. That season, they were scheduled to put on the plays *Excess Baggage, Cradle Snatchers, Laff That Off, The Squall, The Man Who Came Back,* and *Yellow.*

With a new play going up every week, the quality of the productions by stock companies is rarely top-notch. But Cukor's plays were professionally executed and allowed the actors to develop their craft by playing many different characters in a single season. "The constant tension either makes you or breaks you," Bette said later. "Every actor knows that stock can make you slick rather than profound; but you can't play a concerto until you know your scales."

As she developed her skills with the Temple Players, Bette had to modify her habit of being a know-it-all. "You're just a kid, Bette, and there's a great deal you don't know," the actress Dorothy Burgess told her. "Don't be afraid to admit you're wrong."

Everything seemed to be going smoothly in Bette's life. She started dating a young man named Charlie Ainsley, who came to every performance, sent her yellow roses, and took her out to dinner. Reviews of her performances, meanwhile, were excellent and her acting was improving steadily.

But, as always with Bette, a crisis appeared - in this case, a crushing blow. Louis Calhern, the star of the play *Yellow,* objected to having her play his lover because she was so young. "She looks more like my kid than my mistress," he complained.

The problem could have been easily solved with a bit of shuffling of parts; instead, Cukor simply fired her. "I will never really know why," she said later. "He never told me." (Other actors speculated that the real reason was that Bette refused to grant sexual favors to the company's producer, George Kondolf.)

Bette was devastated. But Ruthie would not let her stew about it. She suggested that her daughter get in touch with James Light of the Provincetown Playhouse, who had offered her the role she had quit school for the previous spring. She did, and was delighted that the ingénue spot was still open. But Light - unhappy that Bette had gone off to Rochester rather than wait in New York for his production to start - made her audition for the role.

Audition she did, and was awarded the part, signing a contract for $35 a week. In her roller-coaster life, Bette was on top of the world again. Ruthie found a basement apartment on Eighth Street in Greenwich Village, near the theater on MacDougal Street.

She didn't fully appreciate it at the time, but Bette was about to become part of a grand tradition. Named after the Cape Cod town where the company's original actors and playwrights gathered, the Provincetown Playhouse was already legendary as the theater that introduced Eugene O'Neill to the world. For many, it was "the real birthplace of American drama," in the words of critic William Archer. "I was starting to be frightened," Bette recalled later. "This was the real thing. I had to be good. This was New York - not Broadway, but New York!"

The play Bette would be appearing in was called *The Earth Between*, about a Nebraska farmer named Nat Jennings who harbors an incestuous desire for his seventeen-year-old daughter Floy, played by Bette. It was extremely racy subject matter. Bette, though, was too naïve to figure out what was really going on in the plot. In her closeted upbringing, she had never considered that such a thing was possible - especially since her own father had been so distant. Director Light could see that Bette was clueless but was excited to realize that it was better that way: In rehearsals, she maintained her air of total innocence, to great effect.

When opening night arrived, in March of 1929, the top New York critics were there, including St. John Greer Ervine, Brooks Atkinson, Burns Mantle, and others. So was Ruthie, of course, as well as Bette's friends - plus Charlie Ainsley, her boyfriend from Rochester, who sent her a rose with a note that said, "I love you."

As the play began, its faults were apparent. The script by the up-and-coming playwright Virgil Geddes was "stark, faltering, rigid, and disjointed" in the words of one reviewer. But as the evening progressed, the audience and critics alike succumbed to the power of the Oedipal story: A boy falls in love with Bette's character but her father becomes jealous and throws the boy out of the house and into the barn. When the boy comes down with pneumonia and dies, the father is perversely pleased to have his daughter all to himself.

Later, Bette would remember little of the play itself except for the last scene, when she stood in a wheat field, yielding to her too-affectionate father. "Suddenly there was a clap of thunder and a frightening rumble that vibrated throughout the building," she recalled. "I thought the rain had caused the roof to cave in. It was the audience. It was applause."

The curtain rose and fell so many times during curtain calls that Bette later said it was like a great eyelid, blinking up and down, as the ovation continued. For the rest of her life, she said later, she never again felt as ecstatic as when she returned to her dressing room after the show. There were flowers and telegrams from friends and family, including her sister Bobby from her college in Ohio. A basket of spring flowers with a wicker handle came with a card that bore only an engraved name. It was from her father, Harlow Morrell Davis.

The next day, Bette read the reviews with Ruthie. The one-act that proceeded her play, O'Neill's *Before Breakfast*, was widely panned. *The Earth Between* also got a roasting from Ervine of the *World*, who speculated that the playwright, Geddes, "probably never came into contact with a Nebraskan farmer." But, he added, the play was "remarkably acted, especially by *Miss Bette Davis.*"

Ruthie screamed with joy.

As Bette and her mother riffled through the newspapers looking for her name, they found that one reviewer after another had raved about her performance, including critics from the *News,* the *Graphic,* the *Sun,* the *Telegram,* and *The Brooklyn Eagle*. Ruthie saved *The New York Times's* Brooks Atkinson for last: "Miss Bette Davis, who is making her first appearance, is an entrancing creature who plays in a soft, unassertive style."

Bette fell back onto her pillow, relieved. Ruthie began to cry. After all those years of sacrifice and suffering, they knew she was going to make it. More heartache lay in store for both of them, but from that moment on, there was no question that Bette Davis was here to stay.

# 3

# "YOU WILL SOMEDAY BE KNOWN IN EVERY COUNTRY IN THE WORLD."

After her opening night triumph in *The Earth Between*, Bette began imagining her future. Her dreams now included the ever-supportive Charlie Ainsley, who had just asked her to marry him. As she turned twenty-one during that spring of 1929, she imagined a life of domestic and professional bliss: Living in a romantic cottage, "making a pot of chowder and steamed clams for my husband and then be wafted back to the flower-strewn stage at 8:40."

Like her other suitors, Ham and Hall, Ainsley was tall and lean and utterly devoted to her. But even as she accepted his marriage proposal, she realized that she did not trust her own feelings, which tended to change quickly. "I did adore him," Bette recalled later. "But then, there were other boys I adored. . . . I was bursting with an energy, vitality and passion that I had little understanding of."

Fortunately, her work provided a dependable outlet for her turbocharged emotional life. It could also, however, make her indifferent to the men who pursued her. What did it matter how *they* felt about her when the critics were raving? And then there were the adoring crowds who demanded an extension of the four-week run of *The Earth Between.* Who could resist that?

She was also getting visits from accomplished peers who wanted to work with her. One night after a show, the actor Cecil Clovelly came to her dressing room to speak the words she had dreamed of hearing since seeing her first Ibsen play in Boston as a star-struck teenager: Would she like to go on tour with an Ibsen repertory company and play Hedvig in *The Wild Duck*?

Bette's face lit up. That was the only answer Clovelly needed. The next morning, she met with Blanche Yurka, the celebrated actress currently starring in the play. Linda Watkins, who was playing Hedvig, could not do the road tour, Yurka explained, so they needed a replacement. But first, Bette would have to spend a week in New York replacing Watkins as Bolette in another Ibsen play, *The Lady from the Sea.*

Yurka, a magnetic woman who Bette thought looked like a giant, graceful bird of prey, asked her to read some of Hedvig's lines. When the informal audition was over, Yurka nodded her approval and told Bette she would have one week of rehearsals after closing *The Earth Between.*

Bette was ecstatic as she rode home down Fifth Avenue in the top deck of a double-decker bus. But she immediately came down with the measles and barely made it through her performance that night.

That wasn't her only bit of bad luck. Her emotionally remote father attended the show that night. And he played his part well, unfortunately for Bette. In her dressing room afterward, he began discussing the play in his usual detached, intellectual way, without mentioning his daughter's role, not even once. "Most interesting character analysis," he opined. "Ashburn was excellent . . . that Burgess fellow was very fine . . . and the boy who played Jake conveyed the Cretin-like aspects. . . . Geddes is under the influence of Robinson Jeffers . . . he has power . . ."

Bette was crushed by her father's insensitivity. "We sat looking at each other, strangers," she recalled later. "Just as we'd always been."

She also realized, almost for the first time, how socially awkward and inarticulate he could be. "Would - would you care - to go out with me and have a little supper?" he stammered.

"I'm sorry, Daddy. I feel wretched - really."

He did not believe her. "I see!" he muttered.

"I have a chill and I'm soaking wet."

Unable to convince him, Bette simply said a sad goodbye to her father, went home and collapsed into bed.

When she woke up the next day, still feeling wretched from the measles, Bette was convinced that not only would she be unable to finish the final week of *The Earth Between*, but had surely lost the chance to play the Ibsen roles as well.

Her mother, as always, had other ideas. Ruthie called Clovelly, who called Yurka, who called Watkins. After much discussion, it was agreed that Watkins would continue to play Bolette in *The Lady from the Sea* in the hope that Bette would recover within ten days to play the final few performances of that play and then go on tour with *The Wild Duck*.

Though she was too sick to finish her run in *The Earth Between*, Bette could at least prepare for her Ibsen plays from her bed. So began a miserable ten days as she tried to learn her lines, still feeling awful. She was so weak that reading was difficult. So Ruthie read both plays to her, over and over.

Finally, the day came when Bette was due at the

theater for a 9:30 a.m. rehearsal, followed directly by her performance in *The Lady from the Sea*. Despite arriving an hour late, frantic and apologetic because Ruthie had not properly set the alarm clock, Bette aced the rehearsal. Still weak from her illness, she managed to finish out the last days of *The Lady from the Sea*.

As her health returned to normal, Bette threw herself into final preparations. It would get better from here.

*The Wild Duck* opened in Jackson Heights, Long Island, before going on a tour that would include Philadelphia, Washington, Boston, Newark, and Manhattan. When the curtain fell on opening night, she could tell from the applause they had a hit. "I also knew, inside myself, I was good as Hedvig," she said later. Those feelings were borne out by the high praise Bette received from critics at every stop on the tour. Her rapport with the audience grew, and so did her confidence.

But Bette's professional success would have a deleterious effect on her personal life, a pattern that would repeat itself over and over again. When *The Wild Duck* opened in her hometown of Boston, she arrived at the theater to find a letter from her fiancé on her dressing table. Excitedly, she opened it, then her face fell. The engagement was over, Ainsley wrote. His father disapproved of actresses and said the couple was too young to get married.

He was sorry, hoped she would understand, and said he had no choice, that he was helpless to defy his parents' wishes.

Furious, Bette tore up the note and wondered how she could go on stage that night. In another awful coincidence of timing, her father would be in the audience, along with Ruthie and many friends who had come out to support her; if she failed, the whole world would be there to see it. "Why didn't he fight for me?" she wondered. "He never loved me. Why didn't he talk it over with me? I never want to see him again!"

Finally, Bette gathered herself and decided that she was not going to let anyone or anything ruin a glorious evening. When the curtain went up, she said later, she was relieved to find that the only problems she was concerned about belonged to her character, Hedvig. Her character's concerns, however, were eerily similar to Bette's - at least those she felt as child, when her father abandoned the family. "He'll never come home to us again," Hedvig cries. "I think I'll die from all this! What did I do to him? Mother, you've got to make him come home! . . . Yes, I'll be all right - if only Daddy comes back."

Though everyone who knew Bette understood the resonance of those lines, few were prepared for the torrent of emotion she released that night. "That degree of raw naturalism was extreme, shocking," wrote biographer Ed Sikov in *Dark Victory: The Life of Bette Davis*. She was learning to channel explosive, pent-up feelings in service of her art, a process Bette would refine over the years. "Davis had performed before," Sikov wrote, "but now she was an actress."

When the show ended, the applause was deafening. Yurka, as always, took her solo bow. But this time, as the applause continued, the star came over to take Bette's hand and lead her out to the footlights. Bette was stunned by the honor - even more so when Yurka walked offstage, leaving the young actress alone to soak up the applause from the adoring crowd. There was a standing ovation; some even stood on their seats to cheer. As cries of "Bravo! Bravo!" rang out, Bette began to cry.

"The weight that was Charlie was lifted like a miracle," Bette recalled. "I was alone - onstage and everywhere; and that's the way it was obviously meant to be. . . . It is impossible to describe the sweetness of such a moment. You are at once the indulged beloved and the humble lover. Alone! All those marvelous people. My heart almost burst."

Though her fiancé was gone, something greater had taken his place. In that moment, she realized how much she truly loved being a star. And the audience loved her back. As she put it, "This was the true beginning of the one great, durable romance of my life."

When the Ibsen tour ended, Bette came down from her high and returned to real life. She and Ruthie hopped into their Chevy coupe and drove to Ohio to pick up Bobby, then headed back to Cape Cod for another season of summer stock theater. (Bobby, once again, was relegated to a supporting role as Ruthie continued her quest to make Bette famous.) When Bette showed up for work at the Cape Playhouse, the owner, Raymond Moore, gave her a much better reception than the previous year, when all he could offer was a job as an usher. This time, her own dressing room was waiting for her.

Bette was still the company's ingénue but the summer season was notable for the more mature parts she was also being offered – as when she played a sophisticated woman in *The Constant Wife*. She also began to prove that she was not merely a dramatic actress, excelling in her first comedy, *The Patsy*. And she learned the danger of not being able to separate personal passions from professional ones. In Bernard Shaw's *You Never Can Tell*, she became so enamored of the star, Dodd Meehan, that she couldn't focus and learn her lines. That lead to a caffeine-fueled all-nighter as Ruthie and Bobby helped her learn her part just in time for the opening. She did so well that after the show, a bouquet of flowers was left for her along with a contract for the following summer.

In the fall, Bobby headed back to college to

continue her effort to carve out her own identity while Bette and Ruthie returned to New York, both out of work. Renting a room on East Fifty-Third Street, they were so broke, they often depended on various boyfriends and admirers to take them out to dinner for the only decent meal they managed to eat all day.

But Bette was on the cusp of a big breakthrough - her first Broadway role. Through an agent named Jane Broder, she landed a part in *Broken Dishes*, a new show by the playwright and novelist Martin Flavin. Bette was slated to play Elaine, the daughter of the henpecked Cyrus Bumpsted –performed by the respected fifty-one-year-old Scottish actor Donald Meek - who rebels against his haranguing wife.

When *Broken Dishes* opened at the Ritz Theatre on Broadway in early November of 1929, some quibbled that Flavin – the author of a successful play called *The Criminal Code* – had lowered himself to what they called a "pedestrian comedy." But audiences and critics raved, especially about Meeks and Bette. "I was now a bona fide Broadway actress," she said. "A hit."

And she was finally starting to make some real money, being paid $75 a week – about $1,000 today – that was doubled after three months of the run. The funds allowed Ruthie and Bette to graduate from a single room to an actual apartment, on West Fiftieth Street. Their good fortune had come just in time, the stock market crashed just a week before opening night. Meek showed up for work that day and admitted he had lost everything.

It was ironic that as the crash led to the Great Depression, Bette and Ruth finally had a little money to spare. They went on a spending spree, upgrading their wardrobe in an effort to be as chic as movie stars like Constance Bennett. But Bette's tastes remained simple, and the college-age men who took her out were grateful she was content to dine on eggs and fried potatoes at an inexpensive joint after the show (for a time, her love of potatoes earned her the nickname "Spuds.")

As she became successful, Bette sometimes found it difficult to keep her edge. One night, she came home bragging about how beautifully she had acted. But Ruthie surprised her by saying that she had been in the audience - and begged to differ. "It was your worst performance so far," Ruthie said, adding, "You enjoyed yourself too much."

Bette was upset, refusing to talk to her mother for days. But she knew she was right. "The moment an actor allows a part to take over and just has fun - sails - he never gives as good a performance," she said later. "It's a trap easy to fall into but shows lack of discipline. The audience has paid to see you perform, not have fun."

Besides, you never know who might be watching.

One night, a man representing the famous Hollywood mogul Samuel Goldwyn was in the house scouting her as a possible leading lady in *Raffles*, a film starring Ronald Colman. Though she hated being photographed – and was not interested in going to Hollywood - Bette figured, "Why not?" and agreed to a screen test at the Paramount Studio in Astoria, Queens.

By then, it had been two years since *The Jazz Singer* with Al Jolson had made talkies all the rage in Hollywood. Directors were desperate for actors with good speaking voices and even the most highly regarded theater artists - from James Cagney and Spencer Tracy to Walter Huston and Laurence Olivier - would soon be making the switch to sound films.

Bette did not want to be left behind in this new California gold rush. But the screen test did not go well; Goldwyn was not pleased. Bette was badly made up, had a crooked front tooth, wore unflattering clothes, and was clearly insecure in the new medium. (On the plus side, the experience convinced her to get braces.) "It was brutally clear," she said, "that the movies were not for me."

Not yet, anyway. She still had more dues to pay in the theater - and an old romance to rekindle - before Hollywood would come calling again. In the spring of 1930, *Broken Dishes* completed its long, successful run and Bette returned to the Cape

Playhouse for her third season of summer stock. Once again, Ruthie and Bobby came along to help. One evening, as the three of them were watching a movie in a Hyannis Port theater, Bette let out a cry of surprise. There, four rows in front of them, sat her old boyfriend, Harmon O. "Ham" Nelson Jr.

After the show, they all went back to the family's cottage. Though it had been four years since Bette and Ham had been in touch, they felt like it was yesterday. He was leading a band at a local tavern and had the same hours as Bette, so they saw each other a lot that summer. He attended her plays and was impressed by what an accomplished actress she had become. They went for walks on the beach, took drives, and sat around talking about the future, which still felt uncertain for both of them.

In September, Ham went back to college to finish his final year and Bette went to Baltimore, Maryland, to begin the road tour of *Broken Dishes.* But a week later, in Washington, D.C., she got a call from the show's producer, Oscar Serlin, who said he needed a replacement immediately for another play he was producing, *Solid South,* starring the silent-film icon Richard Bennett.

Bette did not want to leave the tour and her co-star Meek, an adorable man she loved working with. And she would have to learn her part in just ten days, in time for its New York opening. Worse, Bennett, her new co-star, was notoriously difficult to get along with. A well-established actor of sixty, he was the father of three famous actresses – Constance, Joan, and Barbara – and would later become best known for playing Major Amberson in Orson Welles's *The Magnificent Ambersons* (1942).

But Bette liked the play - about the fading aristocracy of the South - and felt she could not turn down the chance to appear on Broadway again. Nervous about her first meeting with Bennett, she arrived at the theater to find him eyeing her suspiciously. "So! You're one of those actresses who think all they need are eyes to act," he sneered. "My daughters are the same."

Bette, having just gotten off an overnight train from Washington, was exhausted and in no mood for abuse. "Mr. Bennett, I'm very happy to return to Washington immediately!" she said.

At that, Bennett laughed and said, "You'll do." After that awkward ice-breaker, she had no more problems with the irascible star.

The same could not be said about the critics and the audience, however. A tremendously talented actor, Bennett was undisciplined and known for outrageous behavior, especially when he felt slighted by a review. Sure enough, when *Solid South* opened, the critics found fault with his portrayal of Major Follensby, the grandfather of Bette's Alabama Follensby.

While Bette and the rest of the cast were praised, Bennett was singled out as delivering "as shoddy an impersonation as a fine player could give" by Percy Hammond of the *Telegram*. Burns Mantle in the *News* thought Bennett's Major was enjoyable to watch "but not a faithful likeness of *any* human being." Other reviews were equally unsparing.

Bennett was so upset by the bad press that the following night, when he could not find a prop, he broke character and yelled into the wings, "Stagehand! My cigar!" Such tantrums happened every night until Bennett completely lost it. At one performance, when the audience failed to laugh at one of his funny speeches, Bennett walked to the front of the stage and bellowed, "I guess I'll have to tell this audience a dirty story to get them to laugh." Then he stormed off the stage.

Bette and another actress, suddenly left alone on stage, were stunned into silence. Eventually, they recovered and continued the scene. But the play itself could not recover from Bennett's outbursts. It closed after just two weeks.

Bette did not stay idle for long, however. Hollywood's demand for actresses was so great that it was only a matter of time before a rising stage star like Bette would be sought out again. This time it was David Werner, a talent scout for Universal Pictures, who had come to a show and was impressed by her performance. He approached Bette, saying he was looking for a female lead for the film version of Preston Sturges's hit play *Strictly Dishonorable.* Would she mind taking a screen test? Bette agreed but held out little hope that this one would be any different than the previous disaster.

With her teeth straightened and in charge of her own makeup and clothes this time, Bette felt much more comfortable during the shoot. Carl Laemmle, the head of Universal, approved of the results and Bette got her big Hollywood break: She was offered a contract paying $300 a week ($4,200 today) with three-month options the first year - that is, if her legs were sexy enough to be cinema-worthy.

Bette had worn a long dress for the screen test so the studio wanted silent footage of just her legs. Humiliated and angry, she raised her skirt slowly as the camera panned up her body. A week later, the decision came back: Her legs had been approved.

It should have been an easy decision for Bette to accept Universal's offer. With *Solid South* shuttered, she was out of work. The studio was offering Bette more than she had ever earned in her life. Now she could finally afford a home for herself, Ruthie, and Bobby.

But Bette loved the theater and was broken-hearted at the idea of leaving it. There was also something strange about the contract. Despite it being the biggest and most complex document she had ever seen, it said nothing about her first film being *Strictly Dishonorable.* The reason, she was assured, was strictly technical. The rights to the script were still being negotiated, the studio reps said, but the part was definitely hers.

Bette was also worried that she might fail in Hollywood, being quite convinced that she did not have that elusive star quality the studios treasured so much. She was a talented actress, for sure, but what about that Hollywood glamour? Even Universal knew it was taking a gamble on this unknown, untested actress.

Finally, Bette decided to sign. What's the worst that could happen? She would make a few films that would help her reputation on Broadway and she could always come home to the theater she loved.

Bette's friends couldn't believe that she signed her career away. Going to Hollywood to compete with Jean Harlow, Greta Garbo, and Claudette Colbert? "You, Bette! Do you really think you'll be given a chance to do anything worthwhile?" one said. Others turned their nose up at Hollywood films they felt were below the artistic standards of New York theater. "Now you've done it. Darling! Don't you know you can't lick them there and you won't want to join them?"

Bette tried not to listen. "They're just jealous," she told herself. "Universal has great plans for me!"

But even before she left New York, a meeting with the studio's publicity men made her nervous about what was in store - and also put them on notice that Bette Davis was not to be trifled with. "Now, about your name," one said.

"What about my name?"

"No glamour," the man replied. "Bette Davis. Ugh!"

"It is spelled with an *e* - instead of a *y*," Bette said. "That's unusual!"

"Doesn't have appeal. Picture names have to excite the public - intrigue 'em. *Bette Davis!* It's a great name for a secretary."

But their suggested alternate made her cringe: Bettina Dawes.

*"Bettina Dawes!"* she cried. "I refuse to be called 'Between the Drawers' all my life!"

The publicity men laughed - this new chick was funny. That ended the discussions about her name, and gained her a measure of respect.

As Bette and Ruthie prepared for their trip out West, they sold their car, sublet their apartment, bought some new clothes, and booked train tickets. At Universal's wood-paneled and red-carpeted New York office, Bette was assured she would never regret her decision. Studio chief Laemmle would make her a star overnight, she was told, starting with the prestige film, *Strictly Dishonorable.*

"Clearly, my future was dazzling," Bette recalled. "I sat wide-eyed, luxuriating in the wonders that were in store for me."

The next day, Bette and Ruthie boarded the train for Los Angeles, excited but terrified. After a stop in Chicago, the train pulled away and Bette had the distinct feeling she would never again see her friends and family in her beloved East Coast.

But she felt better when she remembered the summer after she graduated from high school, when she went to see a fortune teller in York, Maine. The woman shook her head in astonishment and said, "You will someday be known in every country in the world."

At the time, Bette had no idea what the woman could have been talking about. Now, she knew.

# 4

# "I WANTED TO BE AN ACTRESS, NOT A GLAMOUR GIRL."

When Bette and Ruth got off the train in Los Angeles with their wire-haired terrier, Boojum, they could scarcely believe their eyes. They had left New York on a snowy December day in 1930; now, five days later, they had landed in a sun-drenched paradise of palm trees, flowers, and warm ocean breezes.

No sooner had she arrived, however, than the studio served up the first of many indignities for the obscure actress. The studio car that was supposed to pick them up never arrived. So they hailed a cab. At the driver's suggestion, they checked into the Hollywood Plaza Hotel. From their room, they called the studio and were told a driver had gone to the train station but didn't see anyone who looked like an actress. This was not the warm welcome she had imagined. Bette was miffed. "I had a dog with me," she snapped into the phone. "You should have known I was an actress."

Bette was told to report to the studio on Monday, which gave her and Ruthie the weekend to find a place to live. They went to a realtor who took them to a gorgeous home on Alta Loma Terrace – but there was no way they could afford it. "It was the sweetest house I had ever seen in my life," Bette said later, fully furnished and stocked with linens, silver, and china. It even had a grand piano. Outside was a patio from which they could see the famous Hollywood Bowl, with its distinctive arches.

Bette left the house heartbroken. With only enough money to live on until she got her first week's salary – and most of that was already spoken for – they were in no position to rent such a grand place. But Ruthie was determined to give her little girl the home she wanted. So she told Bette she would wire her father for money – not only for the house but a car as well, since in Los Angeles you had to drive to get anywhere. "It's the least he can do at this point," her mother said.

Ruthie had no intention of wiring her ex-husband, but she did have a plan. Next, she took Bette to a Ford car dealership, where they found themselves sitting in a green Model A Phaeton with bright yellow wheels, an adorable vehicle they could also not afford. "You look just right, Bette, sitting at that wheel," the salesman said. To which she wise-cracked, "We'll be sitting in jail if you keep going on this way."

Ruthie pleaded with Bette to borrow money from the studio to pay for the gorgeous house and car, but Bette refused – she would not beg for money before she even put in a day's work. That sparked a screaming match so loud that Ruthie called the hotel front desk to complain about the noise to confuse the management and make sure they didn't get kicked out.

Exhausted, Bette finally went to bed and slept soundly while Ruthie went to Plan B. She got up at five-thirty the next morning to call the Roosevelt Hotel, having heard that an old friend of their family, former Maine governor Carl Milliken, was staying there. When the hotel confirmed that he was a registered guest, Ruthie hung up and ran to the hotel, knowing that Milliken played tennis at seven o'clock every morning.

As he was leaving the hotel for the tennis court, Ruthie arrived, and they both remarked on the amazing coincidence of running into each other. But Ruthie looked worried, so he asked if everything was all right. "I need five hundred dollars immediately," she blurted out, for a car and place to live, since they had just arrived in Hollywood and Bette hadn't been paid yet. What she really needed, she said, was a short-term loan. The kindly ex-governor, his tennis game waiting, pulled out a wad of cash, peeled off five $100 bills, and went on his way.

Ruthie was ecstatic but knew Bette would have a fit if she learned her mother was out begging rich people on the street. So she went straight to Western Union and paid the clerk to write out a phony message from Bette's father. "WIRE RECEIVED. SENDING MONEY NEVER ASK AGAIN. HARLOW M. DAVIS."

Ruthie returned to the hotel and slipped the wire under their door. As Bette was reading it, her mother returned to the room and read it too. Elated, Bette ordered a large breakfast. They bought the car, signed the lease, and moved into their glorious new home. Their first guest was Governor Milliken, who discreetly kept Ruthie's little secret.

Feeling on top of the world, Bette bounced into the studio on Monday morning for her first day of work. As she waited in the reception area for Carl Laemmle, Universal's legendary founder and chief, other executives found excuses to wander in and check out the boss's latest discovery. None seemed impressed. Finally, Laemmle opened his door, and Bette entered.

The bespectacled sixty-four-year-old studio head studied her carefully, looking her up and down.

Photographs and screen tests are one thing, but Laemmle needed to scrutinize her in person, to see exactly what he was paying for. As usual, Bette was wearing no makeup except lipstick. She had never even seen the inside of a beauty parlor, so her hair was not styled in the least – just tied up in a knot in back. Clearly, the boss was disappointed. Afterward, standing in the outer office, she heard him loudly compare her to a tall, gangly male comedian popular at the time: "She has as much sex appeal as Slim Summerville!"

That hurt. "It was a long time after that before I regained my security," she recalled later. "I had been convinced he was right."

After a week of being photographed in various poses – the studio's way of searching desperately for her best angles – Bette was asked to test for a part in a picture. Finally!

But the first sign that something was wrong came when she was not given a script. The next giveaway was when she arrived at the studio and was asked to lie on a couch. Then, to her horror, a parade of male actors entered, one after another, and began caressing her and kissing her on the lips as a director watched. They said ridiculous things like, "You gorgeous, divine darling. I adore you. I worship you. I must possess you." At least fifteen actors, all well-known stars, took turns grabbing her and pulled her close. Often, they ended up lying on top of her.

"Cut!" the director would say after each one. "Who's next?"

This was par for the course in Hollywood for a new actress, but Bette had never heard of anything like it. She was stunned and felt angry, violated. "Aside from my mortification, the fact that I might just as well have been a dummy further enraged me," she said later. "The camera was concentrated exclusively on the men as they ravaged this anonymous thing. From any angle whatsoever, it was disgusting. I wasn't even a woman. I was a mattress in a bawdyhouse."

Only one actor – a young up-and-comer named Gilbert Roland – seemed to realize how shocked she was. "Don't be upset," he whispered as he went through the motions of romancing her, just like the others had. "This is the picture business. We've all gone through it. Just relax!"

If this was the picture business, Bette wanted no part of it. She returned home, miserable. It was late December, but she felt no Christmas cheer. Los Angeles had no snow, only a hot sun and cheap Christmas decorations on Hollywood Boulevard. "I loathed the whole place and cried like a baby," she recalled.

Tied up in a three-month contract, Bette had little choice but to stew and wait for her first role. It was clear from Laemmle's reaction that she was being passed over for *Strictly Dishonorable*, the film promised to her when she signed her contract. But soon enough, she was called in to audition for another film, *Heart in Hand*, starring Walter Huston. It was the debut of director William Wyler, who would later win three Academy Awards and would direct Bette in three films over the next decade – but she didn't get that job, either.

Finally, Bette landed her first role, in a film called *Bad Sister* – but was disappointed to be cast as the bland, but good, sibling. The part had no meat to it. On the plus side, she got to work with Conrad Nagel, whom she had seen on the big screen many times. "I couldn't believe that I was actually sitting next to him on the set," she recalled. (The film also starred a young Humphrey Bogart.)

*Bad Sister*, Bette Davis's screen debut, opened in San Bernardino, south of Los Angeles, in March of 1931. Bette and Ruthie sat in the last row of the balcony, tingling with anticipation. But as the movie progressed, her worst fears were realized: It was awful. So was she. Bette could plainly see that she was not the least bit photogenic. To make matters worse, her smile was lopsided, caused by being embarrassed in front of the camera. "My hair, my clothes, my God!" she thought. When the film was over, mother and daughter drove home in silence.

When her three-month contract expired, Bette was sure that her Hollywood career was over.

So when Laemmle called her into his office, she braced herself for the worst. Instead, he shocked her by renewing her contract for another three months. Later, she found out why: Karl Freund, the cameraman on *Bad Sister*, had spotted one of the very qualities that would eventually make her a huge star:

"Davis," he told his boss, "has lovely eyes."

But Laemmle was still not sold. Far from it. "The kid might be all right in certain roles," Bette was told he said. "But what audience would ever believe that the hero would want to get *her* at the fade-out?"

Once again, Bette felt demoralized. But more insults were on their way: A secretary at Universal, apparently trying to be helpful, explained what her problem was - nobody noticed her. "When Jean Harlow is a mile away, the men sit up and take notice," she told Bette. "You've got to do something about yourself. You've got to look sexy."

Bette was confused. "Was there just one kind of attractive woman?" she wondered. Lots of boys back east had found her lovely, as did theater audiences. Nobody seemed to mind that she didn't look like Jean Harlow. Maybe it was a West Coast thing? "Was I like certain wines?" she wondered. "I couldn't 'travel'?"

What kept her going in those days were funny letters from her long-distance beau, Ham - and the hope that, even in superficial Hollywood, talent might still matter. "When would they all know that I wanted to be an actress, not a glamour girl?"

As she waited impatiently for her next role, Bette realized how easy she'd had it up until now. She had moved quickly from unknown to a promising Broadway actress. Now she was paying her dues – and learning that show business was a fickle beast. That was especially true in Hollywood, where studio bosses cared little for talent, originality, and brains; what they really wanted was a sexy young actress they could mold into an image to sell.

But Bette pulled herself out of her rut by becoming fascinated by movies as an art form. After tedious days of photoshoots in bathing suits and evening gowns, she spent her nights going to theaters and studying what made movies succeed or fail: the scenes, the camera angles, the editing, the dramatic arc of the story. With talkies still in their infancy, directors were conducting intriguing experiments with the new medium, trying to figure out how to maximize its enormous potential.

She also began to understand the difference between stage and film acting. Having a microphone meant she didn't have to project nearly as much. The camera's ability to zoom in for close-ups meant that her movements had to be far more restricted than on stage. As she watched other actors in the darkened theater – Greta Garbo, John Barrymore,

George Arliss, and Ruth Chatterton – she began thinking about ways to modify her technique.

"Once I learned that - unlike the theatre - the slightest purse of the lip, lowering of the lid, vibration of the wrist, could convey what I wished in the Memling canvases of the movies, I tried to open the hearts of the women I played," she said later. "I had to feel my way carefully through the strangeness of the new medium."

She learned to appreciate the artfulness of a well-made film, an insight that changed her life. Suddenly, she felt free. She would strive to become part of the grand tradition of fine acting that began on stage and was now, at this historic moment, migrating into talking films. "Something inside of me told me that this was not the graveyard of my dreams but just a valley I must suffer," she said later. "My despair dissolved into hope."

But her next five movies provided little justification for optimism. In *Seed*, released in May of 1931, and *Waterloo Bridge*, out the following September, she was given small supporting roles that did not register with critics.

Universal, not sure what to do with her, lent her out to other studios for her next three films, none of them memorable. In *Way Back Home*, released by RKO in November of 1931, she was finally cast as a love interest – and actually looked like someone a movie star might want to kiss – but *Variety* called it "unbelievably bad." Her next two films – *The Menace* (Columbia Pictures) and *Hell's House* (Capital Films) – were both made quickly and released within a day of each other in January of 1932 to tepid reviews.

"I was taking a beating all right, but at least I was learning about working on the screen in the process," Bette recalled later. "Each performance had shown some improvement, more confidence, greater ease before the camera." And the public was beginning to take notice. After six films in her first year in Hollywood, she was starting to become a recognizable name, thanks to the fan magazines of the day.

Happy to be working, and gaining confidence, Bette felt that her time had come. But in the summer of 1931, Universal did not pick up her option. After three films and three loaners, they wanted nothing more to do with this headstrong actress who did not fit any conventional definition of how a movie star should look or act.

It was, she would say later, the lowest point in her career. Ever since she left New York, Bette had been fantasizing about returning as a movie star. Now she would limp back home an utter failure. Without a contract, she and Ruthie – and Bobby, who had dropped out of college to join the family in L.A. – would be broke again, once more struggling to survive.

In September of 1931, with heavy hearts, they made reservations for the train back to New York. They packed up their belongings and arranged to sell the car.

Then, like a preposterous Hollywood plot twist, the phone rang.

"George who?" Ruthie said when she answered. "Arliss? Bette, it's for you - it's George Arliss."

Obviously, some friend was playing a prank on her. There was no way a big star like George Arliss could be calling her. Since Arliss was British, Bette playfully adopted a phony English accent: "Yes, Mr. Arliss, and what can I do for you?"

Puzzled, the voice on the other end said, "Is this Miss Bette Davis?"

"Of course," Bette replied, still goofing around. "And how are you, old boy?"

Finally, George Arliss convinced Bette that he really *was* George Arliss. As she listened to the voice ramble on, Bette was nearly speechless.

Arliss occupied a rarified place in the Hollywood ecosystem. The sixty-three-year-old actor had a long and distinguished career on the stages of London and New York before becoming a silent film star in the 1920s, then moved into talkies with 1929's *Disraeli*, for which he won an Academy Award for Best Actor. His stature was such that he had great creative control over his films, including choosing which actors he would work with.

That's why he was calling. As Bette listened, dumbfounded, Arliss explained that he was having trouble casting the leading lady in a new Warner Brothers film called *The Man Who Played God* – a remake of the 1922 silent film of the same name that he had starred in. Murray Kinnell, a British actor who had worked with Bette in *The Menace*, had recommended her. Could she possibly meet him at the Warner Brothers studio in two hours?

"Could I be - try and stop me!" Bette thought. "The sky was blue again. The grass was green. An Arliss picture!"

When she arrived for the meeting, Arliss oozed charm and graciousness. "How do you do Miss Davis?" he said. "*So nice of you to come!* Please sit down."

Instantly, Bette felt at ease. Here was the type of serious theater artist she was used to dealing with in New York. After a few pleasantries, Arliss said, "Tell me, my dear. How long were you on the stage?"

"For three years, Mr. Arliss."

"Hmm!" he said. "Just enough to rub the edges off."

Then he looked at her in a thoughtful, penetrating way. "Universal had asked to see my legs," she thought. "Mr. Arliss was examining my soul."

His gaze seemed to last forever. Finally, Arliss turned away and placed his trademark monocle in his eye. "The part is yours," he said. "Go to the casting office right away. They will take you to the wardrobe department."

Bette was too shocked to move. Eventually, she managed to thank him and leave the office without fainting. When she got to the wardrobe department, she couldn't hold it in any longer. "I can't believe it! I can't believe it!" she screamed, jumping up and down and hugging everyone she saw.

The next morning, Bette went to rehearsal, over-the-moon excited to be working with such a fine cast of actors – Violet Heming, Louise Closser Hale, Ivan Simpson, and Oscar Apfel. Arliss always chose his actors carefully, preferring those with extensive stage experience, so his films had the kind of dignified artistic integrity that in those days was usually found only in theater productions.

*The Man Who Played God* was adapted from a play, *The Silent Voice* by Jules Eckert Goodman, which in turn was based on a short story by Gouverneur Morris. The plot revolves around Montgomery Royle, a famous concert pianist who falls in love with Bette's character, a much younger woman named Grace Blair, before he loses his hearing in an accident. He is devastated but soon learns to lip-read. While gazing out his window with binoculars, he discovers that Grace is having an affair: He watches her explain to her boyfriend that she loves him but could never leave her handicapped fiancé. In the end, Royle nobly releases her from their engagement and makes peace with himself.

During the filming, Arliss made sure Bette's makeup and wardrobe were just right. It was the first time she had ever received such attention on a film set – and it made a huge difference in how she looked on screen. As always, she arrived on time every day, eager and ready to work. "I did not expect anything except a nice little performance," Arliss said later. "But when we rehearsed, she startled me; the nice little part became a deep and vivid creation, and I felt rather humbled that this young girl had been able to discover and portray something that my imagination had failed to conceive."

When the film premiered on February 20, 1932, with all the glamour of a New York opening, it was praised lavishly by critics – though *The Hollywood Reporter* dissented, calling it "clean, wholesome, and dull." But the film finally put Bette Davis on the map, with *The Saturday Evening Post* writing, "She is not only beautiful, but she bubbles with charm."

It was the biggest turning point of her career. After seeing the rushes, Jack Warner was so impressed that he signed Bette to a seven-year contract with Warner Brothers. She would remain with the studio for the next eighteen years. "Ruthie, Bobby and I breathed a sigh of relief," she recalled later.

Finally, their days of scuffling were over.

Bette Davis had arrived.

# 5
# "THE KID IS WALKING AWAY WITH THE PICTURE."

Bette spent her first year in Hollywood playing small roles in forgettable films. But her breakout performance in *The Man Who Played God* meant that her true apprenticeship could now begin.

It would take the Hollywood studios years to discover how to fully exploit her volatile, idiosyncratic talents. In the meantime, Bette was glad to land some roles that were more challenging than a young actress could hope to expect. In *So Big* with Barbara Stanwyck, she played a farm girl who ages into a gray-haired woman. In *The Rich Are Always With Us*, she honed her skills in a drawing-room comedy notable for the glamorous presence of her idol, Ruth Chatterton.

To Bette, Chatterton was both a role model and rival. On her first morning of shooting, the twenty-three-year-old Bette was star-struck by the famous actress, who had recently been nominated for two Oscars. "I had never seen a real star-type entrance in my life," she recalled later. "Her arrival could have won an Academy nomination. Such authority! Such glamour!"

In her first scene with Chatterton, Bette had to approach her in a restaurant. Terrified, she just stood by her table, unable to get a word out. Finally, she blurted out, "I'm so damned scared of you I'm speechless!" That broke the ice; Chatterton helped calm Bette's nerves, and they worked quite well together. It was a lasting lesson: Later, Bette would remember how kindly Chatterton treated her and make it a point to do the same to the younger crop of actresses.

But Bette would soon be heartbroken when Chatterton swooped in to win the affection of their twenty-seven-year-old co-star, George Brent. Bette had met the handsome Irish actor when they appeared together in her previous film, *So Big*. That was the beginning of a long fascination Bette would have with Brent, resulting in an affair a few years later. But at this moment, Chatterton had the inside track. In August of 1932, a few months after filming was complete, the thirty-nine-year-old star divorced her husband and married Brent the very next day.

As Bette shook off that disappointment, her career continued to rise. The quality and frequency of her films increased, and Hollywood took note. She was now compared to stars far more famous. For instance, the lighter shade of blond hair George Arliss had suggested – styled in what she called her "slick coiffure" – made people say she looked like the famous actresses Constance Bennett and Carole Lombard. The fan magazines even published photos of the three of them with captions that said, "Hollywood Look-alikes" and "Couldn't They Be Sisters?" Though somewhat flattering, the comparisons drove Bette crazy. She was desperate to carve out her own identity.

By now, strangers were stopping Bette on the street and sending fan letters. Ruthie was delighted – so proud of her daughter and relieved that their money problems finally seemed to be over. (Bette repaid former Governor Milliken the $500 her mother had borrowed.) They got another house on the ocean at Zuma Beach and bought a stylish luxury car, an Auburn.

And yet, Bette wanted more – not material possessions but the satisfaction and social status that comes with being an acclaimed actress. She knew the industry was fueled by glamour queens, but to her, they were show-biz personalities, not artists: women who looked even phonier next to the gorgeous realism the camera captured when it filmed natural scenery. That's what she wanted – to look as natural as the wilderness, like that other force of nature critics would compare her to, Marlon Brando.

Said Bette, "I strove for reality."

As her notoriety grew, Bette found it difficult to have much of a personal life. She had no lack of suitors, avidly pursued by a creature she derisively called The Hollywood Male. Bette wasn't much interested in these men, being too busy making one movie after another. (She had already appeared in five films in 1932 by the time *The Rich Are Always with Us* came out in May of that year.) She also found the high self-regard of The Hollywood Male a big turnoff. "The male ego with few exceptions is elephantine to start with," she said later. "Add to it a movie contract and it soars through space and into eternal orbit around itself."

An exception was Ham, her on-again/off-again boyfriend with whom she had faithfully kept up a correspondence over all those years. She was excited when Ham wrote to say that he was coming to California soon, right after graduating from college. Ham, as it turned out, had landed a job playing trumpet with an orchestra that would be performing at the 1932 summer Olympics in Los Angeles.

Maybe now, finally, she could strike a healthy balance between her career and her romantic life.

It had been a long time since Bette and Ham had seen each other, but remarkably enough, they picked up right where they had left off. Spending time with Ham felt like being home in New England, and his down-to-earth personality was refreshing in the fake, glitzy world of Hollywood. Their biggest issue was Bette's increasing fame and wealth. Bette tried to make light of it, hoping to set him at ease. But the imbalance in their income and social status clearly made him uncomfortable.

Another problem was Bette's virginity, which she and Ruthie – not to mention Ham – agreed had gone on too long. As always, Ruthie had a solution: "You and Ham have been in love for years. Marry him!"

Bette wasn't so sure. So Ruthie began a fierce campaign to convince her daughter to tie the knot, becoming especially vocal one night at dinner with a group of friends who joined in the lobbying effort. Bette, still too puritan to consider ending her virginity any other way, finally relented. As for the laid-back Ham, she said later, he "was not against the idea."

With that ringing vote of confidence, the very next day Bette, Ham, Ruthie, and Bobby, along with Bette's Aunt Mildred and cousin Donald and two poodles, crammed into a car and drove to Yuma, Arizona for a quickie wedding.

The 275-mile drive seemed to take forever, especially when the thermometer hit 115 degrees. When they finally arrived in Yuma, Bette and Ham were not speaking. Nobody remembers what the fight was about. But she could not have been cheery that her beige dress was drenched with sweat – nor pleased with the limp and wilted gardenias pinned to her lapel. It was a far cry from the image she always had of her wedding day: She had imagined walking down the aisle in a white satin dress with orange blossoms to the music of Mendelssohn.

Nevertheless, on August 18, 1932, the Reverend Schalbaugh of the Indian Mission declared Ruth Elizabeth Davis and Harmon Oscar Nelson Jr. husband and wife. Right after the ceremony, there was no time for revelry: The exhausted bride and groom and their wedding party climbed back into the sweaty car and returned to Los Angeles.

After that inauspicious start, things improved. Bette loved being married. "I felt safe," she recalled later. "I now had the work and the man I loved - the best of two worlds. It never occurred to me that they would or could collide."

But in time, they did.

Until then, though, Bette was eager to settle down after a turbulent childhood with constant moving – Ruthie and Bobby later estimated the family lived in a total of seventy-five different homes. So she and Ham giddily moved into what she called her "dream cottage" - a white, ivy-covered English-style house on Horn Avenue just north of Sunset Boulevard in West Hollywood.

To Bette, home meant not just her husband, but her mother and sister as well. So Ruthie and Bobby moved into a guest house in the back. "I wanted us all to be together," Bette said later. Ruthie was all for it, finding it difficult to let go and allow her daughter to have her own life.

Ham wasn't crazy about living with his in-laws, but the one who suffered the most was Bette's sister. At age twenty-three, after a lifetime of being considered less worthy of attention than her big sister – and also unable to detach herself from her dysfunctional family – Bobby began having severe anxiety attacks. Bette considered her sister's mental health a private family matter and did not publicly discuss it in detail. But some observers have speculated that Bobby suffered from manic depression.

"Bobby's security seemed shattered by my marriage," is all Bette said in *The Lonely Life* about this episode. "She felt she had lost me and her anxieties took on the proportions of a nervous breakdown."

Bobby's mental state was bad enough to make Ruthie consider putting her in a sanatorium. But she couldn't bear being separated from her troubled daughter. So she moved with Bobby to

Dover, Massachusetts, to be near Ruthie's sister Mildred and her husband Myron.

Once they were gone, Bette realized that it was hard to break the habit of constantly moving. She and Ham moved into Greta Garbo's former house on San Vicente Boulevard in Brentwood for a while, then to 906 North Beverly Drive in Beverly Hills. Finally, they settled in at 5346 Franklin Avenue in Los Feliz, a hillside neighborhood in central Los Angeles.

Amid all this turbulence in her personal life – a rushed marriage, Bobby's illness, and constant moving – Bette forged ahead with her career, trying her best to kick it into a higher gear.

There was certainly no time for a honeymoon: Warner Brothers required its stars to take a thirty-two-day, cross-country tour of America to promote its hugely expensive musical, *Forty-Second Street.* With the Great Depression raging, the studio bet – accurately, it turned out – that people would be so eager to escape their misery that they would welcome, rather than resent, the arrival of a gold-leafed Pullman train full of glamorous stars. (One car was even turned into a mobile beach scene complete with sand, water, and suntan lamps.)

"Bewildered and exhausted as I was by the madness of our caravan, I learned once and for all how much movies mean to the American people," Bette said later. "I arrived back in Hollywood with a greater sense of dedication than ever."

Back in Los Angeles, Bette got down to work. Warner Brothers ran her so ragged that she would appear in a total of nine releases in 1932 alone. Most mornings, she would leave the house at 6:30 a.m. and work into the early evening, at least. That left her little time to see Ham, who didn't return home from his orchestra work until 4:00 a.m.

The quality of her roles gradually improved, and Bette began to feel she was approaching the status that she had dreamed of – being offered plum roles with great directors. In the comedy *The Dark Horse*, she had a ball playing a political operative who tries to get a dim-bulb candidate elected governor. Then, Darryl Zanuck, head of production for Warner Brothers, assigned her to play Madge, the rich, vampish Southern girl in *The Cabin in the Cotton,* which she called "my best role to date."

*The Cabin*'s director, Michael Curtiz, objected to her casting, however, and made her life miserable. As she performed her scenes, Bette could hear the director muttering behind the camera, "God-damned-nothing-no-good-sexless-son-of-a-bitch!" This would put her in the foulest of moods when she got home to Ham, straining their young marriage.

"Heaven help me, I came home ready to explode,"

she said later, "and I often did."

Nevertheless, Bette persevered through the shooting and loved playing the nasty Madge. The critics enjoyed it, too. The *New York American* called her "superb" and the *New York Herald Tribune* said, "Miss Davis shows a surprising vivacity as the seductive rich girl." (One of her favorite lines in the film was quoted widely, even after her death, appearing in the 1995 comedy, "Get Shorty": "Ah'd love to kiss you, but ah just washed mah hair!")

Bette was thrilled that she had found her niche as an actress. "Madge in *The Cabin in the Cotton* was my first downright, forthright bitch," she said later. She hoped it meant she had forever put behind her "the sweet, drab sister type that had plagued me since my arrival."

But Warner Brothers didn't seem to understand how to best use her mercurial talents. Bette was so unlike any actress the studio had seen before; she didn't fit into any of the cookie-cutter roles the film industry loved to squeeze women into: glamour girl, plain-but-sweet girlfriend, devoted wife, etc. In her next effort, a crime drama called *Three on a Match*, she played a less-than-colorful stenographer. The film was poorly reviewed – "tedious and distasteful" according to *The New York Times* – and was directed by Mervyn Le Roy, another man who didn't care for her. Male directors seemed to resent an assertive woman like Bette, who resisted all efforts to control her.

Things went from bad to worse when she was put in another 1932 Michael Curtiz film, *Twenty Thousand Years in Sing Sing.* But by this time, she had become used to Curtiz's dismissive attitude. She was just happy to be playing the moll and thrilled that her criminal love interest was Spencer Tracy, one of the few actors she idolized. But her next film, *Parachute Jumper*, with Douglas Fairbanks Jr. gave her yet another insignificant role – the mistress of a racketeer – and she complained to Jack Warner that the studio was not doing enough to further her career.

Feeling overworked and underappreciated, Bette took out her frustrations on Ham and their maid, Dell Pfeiffer, who did all the cooking and cleaning at home. Pfeiffer, despite enduring what she called Bette's "disturbances," became one of her boss's closest confidants over the next twenty years. "There were battles," Bette said later. "Our little brown-shingled cottage was the scene of many a war. I worried about my stagnant career twenty-four hours a day. And I brought my worries home with me."

Fortunately, George Arliss came calling again, for a comedy called *The Working Man.* This time, playing the spoiled daughter of Arliss's character, she was not nearly as intimidated by the great actor. (After a few days of shooting, he said, "My little girl isn't afraid of me any more, is she?")

From Arliss, she learned how to handle the maddening process of filming scenes out of sequence. "Always keep the continuity in your head," he told her. "It will help." Remembering the pitch of her voice and her moods in previously shot scenes allowed her to make sure they blended well with the scene she was working on.

Because Bette looked reasonably attractive as the love interest in *The Working Man*, released in April of 1933, Warner production chief Zanuck became convinced that the studio should turn her into a glamorous star. "It was a great mistake," she said. That just wasn't who Bette Davis was, but the conventional minds at Warner Brothers – having tried her in most of the other stock female roles – figured they had little to lose, and possibly much to gain, by trying to sell her as a sexy siren.

The futility of this exercise was clear in her next film, *Ex-Lady*, which she called "a piece of junk." Because Hollywood had yet to strictly enforce the Motion Picture Production Code to censor its films, *Ex-Lady* director Robert Florey was free to include such risqué touches as extramarital affairs, the use of birth control, and a revealing negligee worn by the seductive young star Bette Davis. The film was "an ecstasy of poor taste," Bette said later. She would not remember much about the experience itself except the promotional billboards that showed her half-naked. “My shame,” she said, “was only exceeded by my fury.”

Compounding Bette’s frustration was the fact that, under the oppressive contracts of the Hollywood studio system, actors had no say whatsoever in what films they appeared in, what roles they played, even what makeup or costumes they wore. So if Warner Brothers decided Bette was now a glamour queen, there was nothing she could do about it. “Our contracts were outrageous and the security I had dreamed of on Broadway had become the safety of a prison,” she complained.

But her professional problems suddenly took a back seat to urgent personal issues. Bette learned she was pregnant. She was thrilled by the news, but Ham was not. “You’re much too busy to have a baby,” he told her. “It would be stupid to jeopardize your career!”

Another factor in Ham’s reaction had nothing to do with Bette’s best interests: He still felt humiliated about the imbalance in their incomes. Her salary of $1,000 a week (about $18,000 today) was ten times greater than his. Ham wouldn’t even agree that they would buy a house together until he could afford to pay for it himself. Now to have a child? Who would pay for it? “You don’t think I’m going to have *you* pay the hospital bills for the baby,” he indignantly told his wife.

Bette was shocked. They had plenty of money – what difference did it make who paid the bills? She complained to Ruthie, still living in Massachusetts with Bobby, and was surprised to find her mother siding with her husband. She argued that having a baby could seriously derail her career.

Bette was torn. She understood that Ham wanted to provide financially for his child. She also worried about her career, which seemed just about to take off. "I saw everyone's point," she recalled. "I understood everything intellectually. I was wretched emotionally."

In her memoir, Bette does not go into detail about those emotions or explain how she arrived at the difficult decision to have an abortion. She also does not say how it felt to go through the procedure and live with the consequences. All she said was, "I did as I was told."

When she got back to work, Bette found that Warner Brothers was still obsessed with turning her into a glamour girl. In *Fashions of 1934*, a comedy with musical numbers by the legendary Busby Berkeley, she had to wear a platinum wig, false eyelashes, and slinky clothes. "The bossmen were trying to make me into a Greta Garbo," she fumed. In an interview with the fan magazine *Photoplay*, Bette complained, "I can't get out of these awful ruts. They just won't take me seriously. Look at me in this picture - all done up like a third-rate imitation of the MGM glamour queens. That isn't me."

Things did not get better with her next two films, *The Big Shakedown* and *Jimmy the Gent*, which were known as "programmers" – films made for the masses solely to make money. After making a staggering twenty movies in just three years – most of them inconsequential fluff – Bette was feeling burned out.

Taking matters into her own hands, she decided to push hard for a role she had been coveting for a long time. While filming *Twenty Thousand Years in Sing Sing*, she had read *Of Human Bondage*, W. Somerset Maugham's semi-autobiographical novel. She loved it. Learning that RKO owned the film rights, she spent months lobbying Jack Warner to loan her out. Both Maugham and the film's director, John Cromwell, thought she would be perfect. But Warner refused to approve the deal, fearing that having Bette play Mildred Rogers, a cruel and vulgar waitress, would ruin the glamorous image he had been trying to construct for her.

Unlike today, actors of this era did not have high-powered agents who could threaten and intimidate to get their way. So Bette was on her own. Every day for six months, she showed up at Warner's office to plead her case. "I begged, implored, cajoled," she said. "The part of Mildred was something I had to have."

Still, Warner refused. To appease her boss, Bette didn't throw any tantrums when he assigned her the relatively small part of a spoiled, wealthy socialite in the throwaway flick *Fog Over Frisco*. That seemed to help, and Warner began to waver. Finally, he relented, but only after he found a way to make it work for the studio: Warner wanted to use RKO contract player Irene Dunne for the film version of the Jerome Kern-Oscar Hammerstein II musical *Sweet Adeline*, so the studios agreed to trade actresses. Bette didn't care how it happened. At last, she had a great role she could sink her teeth into.

Mildred Rogers was not a character many actresses wanted to play. She was so vile and unlikable that Dunne, Katharine Hepburn, and Ann Harding had all turned down the role. But Bette saw huge potential in the part – it was a great way to show off her range.

Her first challenge was learning a cockney accent, so she hired an English housekeeper and studied her closely to get all the nuances right. A wise move as it turned out. When filming began, her co-star Leslie Howard was cold to her, upset that a British actress had not been chosen. As the shoot progressed, however, he became impressed by her work. He became much friendlier when someone told him, "The kid is walking away with the picture."

Cromwell, meanwhile, did not direct her in a bossy way, allowing her the freedom to construct the character. "I trusted her instincts," he said later. One of those instincts was to reject the current fashion of making even death scenes glamorous; instead, she realistically portrayed her character's devastating final stages of tuberculosis. "I made it very clear that Mildred was not going to die of a dread disease looking as if a deb had missed her noon nap," she said.

Bette played nasty Mildred with such a vengeance that people on the set were shocked. "You gimpy-legged monster!" she screams at Leslie Howard's character, Phillip Carey, who has a club foot. "Do you know what you are? A cripple! A cripple, cripple!" She was so convincing that she even spooked herself and felt ashamed at how evil she could be.

"My understanding of Mildred's vileness - not compassion but empathy - gave me pause," she said. "I barely knew the half-world existed. I was still an innocent."

Nervous about how audiences would react to the film, Bette did not attend a preview in Santa Barbara. But her mother and husband did. For eighty-three agonizing minutes, Ruthie and Ham sat watching Bette spew venom at the other actors. They said not a word, exchanging only brief glances from time to time. When it was over, they left the theater in silence. Later, Ruthie said, "Neither of us knew what to think, for we felt the picture would make or break her, but would the public like the unpleasant story as well as the people at the preview seemed to?"

*Of Human Bondage* premiered in New York City at Radio City Music Hall in June of 1934 and went into general release the following month. Reviewers were ecstatic. *The New York Times* said Leslie Howard's performance "excels any performance he has given before the camera." Meanwhile, *Life* Magazine out-praised all others by calling Bette's performance the greatest ever recorded on screen by an actress.

"It is an interesting fact that most people believe that *Of Human Bondage* was my first picture, although I had made twenty-one films before it," Bette said later. "All these pictures and my parts in them seemed to blend into one colorless glob with a few exceptions."

Not anymore.

*Of Human Bondage* was shot in black and white. But up on the big screen, Bette Davis stood out as if she alone were brightly lit with color.

# 6

# "ONCE AND FOR ALL, I HAD TO CONSOLIDATE MY POSITION AS AN ACTRESS - AND NOT A PAINTED PUPPET SUBJECT TO MY MASTERS' WHIMS."

The rave reviews of Bette's performance in *Of Human Bondage* weren't welcomed by her bosses, who were embarrassed that their contract star was being celebrated for work at another studio. (The Warner Brothers execs even scrubbed any mention of the film from her publicity materials.) Bette suspected that Warner saw her convincing portrayal of the shrew Mildred Rogers as proof of what a pain she could be in real life: "Well!" she imagined them saying. "RKO knew what type of girl she *really* was."

By this time, Bette was well into a tumultuous period in her relationship with the studio, leading to a nasty legal battle that would reverberate throughout the industry. And her spectacular performance in *Of Human Bondage* only served to bring the conflict into high relief.

Tensions flared during the Academy Award season of 1935. Bette, and most of Hollywood for that matter, were sure that she would be nominated for an Oscar – and were shocked when she was not. It was deeply perplexing – outrageous to some. (*Entertainment Weekly* would later rank it as one of the worst Oscar snubs ever.)

Was a conspiracy afoot?

Bette seemed to think so, alleging in her memoir, *The Lonely Life*, that Warner Brothers had put the word out to its personnel who were voting members of the Academy of Motion Picture Arts and Sciences to cast their ballots for anyone but her.

As the uproar grew, a campaign was launched to have Bette nominated anyway; the uprising was even joined by Norma Shearer, also nominated as Best Actress for *The Barretts of Wimpole Street*. The furor led to an announcement by the president of the Academy, Howard Estabrook, that voters could write in their own choices for each award – the first time that had ever been allowed. It also led to the hiring of the accounting firm Price Waterhouse to count the votes and assure their integrity, a practice that continues today.

On awards night in February, Claudette Colbert took home the Best Actress statuette for the Frank

Capra comedy *It Happened One Night*. But the write-in campaign had an effect, propelling Bette to a third-place finish behind Shearer. "I cannot say I wasn't crushed once I had been that close to the prize," she said later. "I had not lost my loathing for [losing]."

Even before the Oscars dust-up, soon after Bette had completed filming *Of Human Bondage* in early 1934, Warner Brothers seemed intent on putting Bette back in her place by casting her in yet another awful movie, *Housewife*, a film so bad she once described it as a "horror." In it, she played not the housewife, but the husband's former flame who returns to stir things up. "I was made to trudge through the professional swamp at Warners brimming over with frustration and rage," she recalled later. "One skirmish after another followed."

Production of *Housewife* was scheduled for April 11 to May 7, 1934, but Bette, fed up with her bosses, did not show up on schedule. It took a series of telegrams from Warner Brothers, reminding her that she was legally bound to play the roles the studio gave her, before she finally arrived on the set a week late.

Her next assignment was a supporting role in another forgettable film, a murder mystery called *The Case of the Howling Dog*. It was almost as if her studio was punishing her for demanding good roles. This time, she not only refused the role but did not respond to calls and wires from studio executives as they tried to get her to comply. When Jack Warner called one day, Ham told him his wife was busy and would call him back. She never did.

Furious, Warner replaced her with an ingénue named Helen Trenholme and put Bette on suspension. The timing was in her favor, however: *Of Human Bondage* had just been released and was receiving stellar reviews. Knowing how foolish he would look if he continued to confine his talented starlet to less substantial roles, Warner relented, reinstated her, and cast her in a melodrama called *Bordertown*, a film that allowed her some dramatic range (and was eventually well-reviewed.)

Now that Bette had tasted what she called "cinematic art" in *Of Human Bondage*, there was no keeping her down on the farm. "I was more and more impatient with the inanities at my studio," she recalled later.

When *Bordertown* started filming, Bette played a scene where she wakes up in bed. As committed to realism as ever, she smeared cream on her face and messed up her hair before getting into the bed. Production was halted for four hours as director Archie Mayo and Bette got into a screaming match over it, with Mayo insisting that Bette look more appealing for the audience. "They still didn't know that I didn't care if I didn't look alluring when I shouldn't," she said later.

Bette won that battle, but there were more to come. When her character, Marie Roark, kills her husband and frames someone else, she is called to testify at the trial and literally goes insane on the witness stand. Mayo wanted her to overplay the scene, but Bette argued that in real life, the clues that someone is crazy are more subtle.

"They'll never know you're supposed to be insane," the director fumed. So Bette offered a deal: If preview audiences didn't understand that she was crazy, she would re-shoot the scene. So they shot it her way, and the preview audiences said they could clearly tell she was nuts.

Her battles weren't confined to the set.

Back at home, her husband did not lend Bette a sympathetic ear when she complained about the way the studio was treating her. She found Ham passive, dull, and totally uninterested in her daily battles on the set. Furious, she would jump into the car and drive hundreds of miles, just to get away from him.

Once again, Bette felt that her career success was coming between them. Ham seemed utterly debilitated by the fact that he wasn't the primary breadwinner "The whole alliance had been a mistake," she said later, "based as it was on economic imbalance."

With her marriage on the rocks, the

twenty-seven-year-old Bette became interested once more in George Brent. After making *So Big* and *The Rich Are Always with Us* with her three years earlier, Brent had more recently appeared with Bette in *Housewife*. Now, in 1935, they made two more films together – *Front Page Woman* and *Secret Agent* (Brent would eventually become her most frequent male co-star, appearing in a total of thirteen films with her).

In her memoir, Bette is coy about exactly when their affair started, saying only that the gossip about them during this time was "not without some foundation." But since Brent was still married, she added cryptically, "He still belonged to Miss Chatterton. My little white cottage might have been in a state of disenchantment, but that is crooked poker in my book." In other words, she would mess around with Brent but was not ready to break up two marriages over him.

Warner Brothers, meanwhile, still had no clue about how to best use their demanding, irascible star. No matter how bad the film, Bette still delivered outstanding performances and the critics and public seemed far more enthusiastic about her than her own bosses did. Part of this was clearly a personality clash, and Bette deeply resented the condescending, paternalistic way they treated her. She did not socialize much with the Hollywood crowd, but when she did, she would sometimes run into Jack Warner at a party. "Remember, Bette," he would say, wagging his finger like an overbearing parent. "You have to be at the studio at six o'clock. Get to sleep soon."

Finally, Warner Brothers found the right role for Bette, one that would produce her first Academy Award. *Dangerous* was the tale of a prominent New York architect who breaks off his engagement after falling in love with Bette's character, the down-and-out actress Joyce Heath who destroys herself with booze and drugs.

Bette hesitated. She found the script maudlin and pretentious. Yet, she was drawn to the character of Joyce partly because she was based on one of Bette's real-life idols, the stage actress Jeanne Eagels. When Warner Brothers production chief Hal B. Wallis convinced her that she could make Joyce a truly memorable character, Bette agreed.

But nothing was easy when it came to Bette.

In fact, during the filming of *Dangerous,* one of Hollywood's greatest feuds was born. It all started when Bette fell in love with her leading man, the tall, dark and handsome Franchot Tone. The suave thirty-year-old actor, hailing from a well-off New York family, would soon be nominated for an Oscar for the recently completed *Mutiny on the Bounty.* "Everything about him reflected his elegance, from his name to his manners," Bette gushed later.

Tone apparently returned Bette's affection. Harry Joe Brown, one of the producers of *Dangerous*, later reported that during the filming, he accidentally caught Davis and Tone in a compromising position.

There was just one problem: Tone was already deeply involved with Joan Crawford, one of the biggest sex symbols of the day, who had recently divorced Douglas Fairbanks Jr. "He was madly in love with her," Bette said of Tone. "They met each day for lunch. After lunch, he would return to the set, his face covered with lipstick. He made sure we all knew it was Crawford's lipstick. I was jealous, of course."

To Bette, Crawford was one of those Hollywood "glamour queens" she looked down upon, women who were successful because of their looks, not their acting ability. Never considered a raving beauty, Bette had to work hard for everything she achieved and resented Crawford for allegedly sleeping her way to the top. Rumors were rife that Crawford cavorted not only with men, but with women, too, including Greta Garbo, Marlene Dietrich, Barbara Stanwyck, and later Marilyn Monroe. Some have even speculated that Crawford was in love with Bette and their feud was inspired by Bette's rejection of her (by all accounts, Bette was heterosexual).

During the filming of *Dangerous*, Crawford and Tone announced their engagement. Bette was furious. Shortly after the shoot wrapped, the couple married in New Jersey. Bette, many say, never forgave Crawford, even though Crawford divorced Tone four years later. ("She took him from me," Bette, then almost eighty, told the journalist Michael Thornton in 1987, two years before her death. "She did it coldly, deliberately and with complete ruthlessness. I have never forgiven her for that and never will.")

Their feud even spilled over into the Academy Awards ceremony in March of 1936. It should have been a thrilling night for Bette when she was announced as the surprise winner of the Best Actress trophy for *Dangerous*. But Crawford was eager to spoil the moment. Never imagining that she would win, Bette had worn a simple navy-and-white checked dinner dress to the ceremony. When her name was announced as the winner, her ex-lover Tone – seated with Crawford directly in front of Bette – rose to congratulate her, but his wife remained sitting. When Tone urged Crawford to congratulate her, the vindictive star – perfectly coiffed and wearing a dazzling evening gown – turned her head, looked her rival up and down, and said, "Dear Bette! What a lovely frock."

The moment was also dampened by Bette's realization that she hadn't really earned the award. "I knew, everyone knew," she said, "that it was a 'Please forgive us for not giving you the Oscar last year when you should have had it for your performance as Mildred in *Of Human Bondage*.'"

There was no doubt, she added, that Katharine Hepburn deserved the award for a spectacular performance in *Alice Adams*. Ruthie and Ham were there to cheer Bette on, but as she made her way to the stage that night to accept the trophy, she couldn't help thinking, "It's a consolation prize."

Still, she had an Oscar. Nobody could take that away from her. A month shy of her twenty-eighth birthday, she had made twenty-eight films and now, finally, was being recognized as an artist by her peers. "I had reached the top of the heap and stood holding the statue while my family glowed with pride," she recalled. "I had done it. I had my career and I still had Ham."

For now, anyway. But both were on thin ice. Her marriage was at least functional, if tormented, but her career had become a crazy roller-coaster ride. After appearing in a prestige film, *The Petrified Forest*, which made Humphrey Bogart a star, and then winning an Oscar, Bette thought she was on a roll. She couldn't wait to see what marvelous film Warner Brothers would offer her next.

The script she was handed, however, was a lame comedy called *Golden Arrow*, which teamed her up again with George Brent. After shooting, Warner Brothers rushed to release the film to capitalize on Bette's Academy Award, despite the fact that it did poorly in audience previews. Such a craven move rankled Bette. "I was actually insulted to have to appear in such a cheap nothing story," she said.

So when her next assignment was *Satan Met a Lady* – an uninspired adaptation of Dashiell Hammett's novel *The Maltese Falcon* (remade into a classic five years later by Bogart and director John Huston) - Bette decided she'd had enough. She was so upset by the vapid script that she marched into Jack Warner's office and demanded better material. Warner assured her that if she would just agree to do this film, he would make sure her next project would be wonderful – honest. Reluctantly, she agreed. Sure enough, the film was a stinker, with *The New York Times* critic Bosley Crowther, saying it "deserved to be quoted as a classic of dullness."

Fully expecting Warner to live up to his promise, Bette hit the roof again at the next part she was given, in a film called *God's Country and the Woman.* Her role would be Jo Barton, a female lumberjack whom Bette called "an insufferable bore who scowled while everyone kept yelling 'Timber!'" This is how she was being treated? After paying her dues for five years in Hollywood, making thirty-one films, most of them duds? And getting two Academy Award nominations and one Oscar?

For the first time in her career, Bette put her foot down and simply refused to play the part. "This was the moment of truth," she said later. "It was the time for real action - an open break, a war in which one of us would win. If I never acted again in my life, I was not going to play in *God's Country*. It was now a matter of my own self-respect."

Another sore spot for Bette was money. She made $18,200 in 1935 – about $328,000 today – which was certainly a great payday in a country still reeling from the Great Depression. But that same year, Warner Brothers had paid actress Kay Francis, who had won no Oscars, $115,000 or $2.1 million today. Paul Muni was making $50,000 per film and was also given the right to approve the story, the part, and the script. Unlike Bette, he was loaned out only with his consent and could do a stage production whenever he wanted. Warner Brothers star James Cagney also had a huge $150,000 salary – and was unhappy with it, knowing how much his star power contributed to his films' success at the box office.

Though Warner Brothers had previously given some of its stars more freedom to choose their projects and collaborators, it soon changed its mind when some of those films did not do well. So it took a bottom-line approach to all its films, churning them out like sausages and paying only lip service to artistic integrity. Speaking for many of her peers, Bette said, "I was beginning to feel like an assembly-line actress."

Bette was not the only one fighting back. Cagney had gone to court against Warner Brothers, too.

Katharine Hepburn (RKO), Margaret Sullivan (Universal), Carole Lombard (Paramount), and Eddie Cantor (Sam Goldwyn) were also feuding with their bosses. But the studios – Warner Brothers in particular – had an ace in the hole that always allowed it to prevail: Standard contracts gave them the power to extend the contract by whatever time period the actor refused to work. So stars who rebelled were merely extending their servitude - high-paying servitude, to be sure, but a hopeless trap nonetheless.

Actors had little choice but to sign these oppressive contracts since the studios had a monopolistic grip on the movie business. But in February of 1936, the federal government finally decided to do something about it: The U.S. attorney general filed a suit against Warner Brothers, Paramount, and RKO for conspiring to monopolize interstate commerce by controlling production and distribution of motion pictures while, at the same time, owning a significant portion of the theaters and bullying the smaller independents. The battle would drag on until 1948, when the Supreme Court finally ruled against the studios, breaking up the monopoly by forcing them to sell their theaters.

In the summer of 1936, with Bette still in the middle of the seven-year contract she had signed with Warner Brothers four years earlier, she demanded a new deal. She asked for a one-year contract, with the option to renew for five years, at a salary of $100,000 for the first year ($1.75 million today) and gradually rising to $220,000 for the fifth ($3.8 million today). She would be required to make no more than four films per year, get three consecutive months of vacation, and be free to work for other studios during her time off. She also wanted her workday to end at 6:00 p.m. If her terms were not met, she would continue to refuse to work.

Soon enough, Bette received a firm answer from Jack Warner. He suspended her for three months.

Like the other studios, Warner Brothers steadfastly refused to set a precedent that would undermine the iron-fisted control they had over their talent. The press had a field day with the battle, with some calling Bette a hero for standing up to her oppressors and others casting her as a greedy, spoiled star throwing a tantrum. Some predicted that Bette would destroy her career.

Unfortunately for Bette, there were no producers in the United States willing to hire the rebellious star and face a legal showdown with Warner Brothers. There was an Italian willing to take that risk, however - the producer and actor Ludovico Toeplitz, who had worked on the 1933 film *The Private Life of Henry VIII* and whose company had produced the 1936 movie, *The Beloved Vagabond.* Toeplitz flew to California to meet Bette and offer her roles in not one but two movies: *I'll Take the Low Road*, to be filmed at Ealing Studios in London, and a second, costarring the French actor Maurice Chevalier, to be made in France. She would get script approval, and he would pay her handsomely: £20,000 per movie, around $50,000 ($900,000 today).

This was just what Bette needed to break the logjam. She readily agreed, and she and Ham quietly traveled to Montreal, then sailed for Scotland. From Glasgow, they traveled to Liverpool, then London, taking a room at Claridge's hotel. There, as Bette suspected, she was served with an injunction from Warner Brothers to prevent her from making the films with Toeplitz.

Because the studio had offices in Great Britain, the matter would go before the British courts. The legal battle was on, but Bette seemed unfazed, happy to be traveling to exotic lands as if it were a vacation, hoping to re-ignite her spark with Ham, and utterly confident that she was right and would win.

"The Scottish press called me an 'unemployed movie star'; and welcomed me with a warmth and a recognition that surprised and did not displease me," she said. "I had not realized how well known I was abroad."

But Warner Brothers was about to strike back, no matter how popular Bette was.

Jack and Ann Warner, flew to Wales and stayed

at St. Donat's Castle owned by the legendary media baron William Randolph Hearst as the studio plotted its legal strategy. Ann Warner diplomatically suggested to her husband that he settle the case. She liked Bette, as did Jack, despite all their arguing, and didn't want her husband marred by bad publicity. But for the studio mogul, the lawsuit was a matter of principle: If Bette won, the entire Hollywood system could come crashing down. Bette was equally resolute. "Once and for all I had to consolidate my position as an actress," she said, "and not a painted puppet subject to my masters' whims."

Meanwhile, her high hopes of rekindling her romance with Ham were dashed. Not long after they settled into the Park Lane Hotel, he told Bette he was heading back to the States: With Bette no longer drawing a salary from Warner Brothers, the Toeplitz films on hold during the court fight, and mounting travel expenses and legal fees, money was tight. He thought it best to find work as a musician in New York. When he boarded a ship in Southampton, Bette felt abandoned, upset at having to face her battle with the studio alone. "It wasn't often I needed him," she said later. "This was the only time."

The legal war, Warner Brothers Pictures, Inc., v. Nelson, (Bette's married name) was waged October 14-16, 1936, in the High Court of Justice,

King's Bench Division. Bette's lawyer, Sir William Jowitt, argued that Warner Brothers caused a breach of contract when it "required [Bette] to play unsuitable parts and had frequently required her to work" for up to fourteen hours a day and to "make an unreasonably large number of films in 1935." Because of this breach, Jowitt contended, she should be free to work for others. The contract, he added, was "a life sentence."

On the other side, the lawyer for Warner Brothers, Sir Patrick Hastings, chided Bette in front of the judge, saying, "I think, m'lord, this is the action of a very naughty young lady." He suggested that Toeplitz had likely bribed Bette and she had accepted for the sole purpose of freeing herself from Warner Brothers. Her contract was the industry standard, Hastings said, rebuking Bette for whining about the terms as her salary continued to climb.

When Jack Warner took the stand, Bette had never seen him so nervous. "For a split second," she said later, "I felt sorry for him." During questioning, he offered some concessions. "I admit," he said, "that an actress could become heartbroken if she had to play parts that were not fitted to her." He also admitted under questioning that, yes, Bette *could* be forced to eat oatmeal for a commercial tie-in if the studio deemed it necessary.

Later, Bette's attorney said it ultimately did not matter how much these movie stars make: "If they are forced as punishment not to work and therefore eventually to starve - that is the question of slavery. I suggest that the essence of slavery is not that it is less slavery because the bars are gilded, but because some authority says, 'You must continue to work under contract.'"

The court wasn't swayed. A contract is a contract, and Bette clearly broke it by signing with Toeplitz. Warner Brothers was granted a three-year injunction, or the duration of Bette's contract, whichever ended up being shorter. So if the studio chose to exercise its options, Bette would be stuck with Warner Brothers for six more years, until 1942.

Bette was stunned by the court's decision. At the most, she was expecting a one-year injunction. "Everyone had warned me not to fight," she said later. "Well, I paid for it. I not only lost the case but a fortune in salary. I owed Sir William his retainer and I was obliged by law to pay Warners' costs, which were tremendous. . . . There was nothing, no positive aspect, I could cling to at all."

Bette decided to appeal. She called Ruthie and asked her to come to England to help her gear up for another fight. The case had already cost her over $30,000 ($525,000 today) and the appeal would cost another $20,000. For days, while she waited for Ruthie, she took long walks on the beach near her hotel. "I wanted to be alone," she said later. "I wanted to think. I was exhausted."

One day, she returned to her hotel to find her old British friend George Arliss in the lobby waiting for her. They sat down for tea. "Go back, my dear Bette," he told her. "You haven't lost as much as you think. Go back gracefully and accept the decision. See what happens. I think good things. If in time you feel you're being treated unjustly, put up another fight. I admire your courage in this affair but now - go back and face them proudly."

Bette realized that he was right - and she was grateful. Arliss had always been like a guardian angel, and he had come through once again. Bette cabled Ruthie to stay in New York. She would be coming home.

By now, Bette was still only twenty-eight years old, in the prime of her career. But by the time she freed herself from her Warner Brothers contract, she could be thirty-four – an "old woman" by Hollywood standards, she told the press. In early November, she set sail for America, sad, angry, deeply in debt, and wondering whether she even had a career left to come back to.

# 7

# “I WAS NEVER SURER OF MYSELF PROFESSIONALLY THAN AT THIS MOMENT.”

As Bette sailed back to America, bitter and defeated, she could not have imagined what a positive impact her legal battle with Warner Brothers would have – both on her fellow actors and her own career.

The episode had cast a harsh spotlight on the Hollywood studio system. It also paved the way for another lawsuit, filed by *Gone With The Wind* star Olivia de Havilland, in 1943, which resulted in the overturning of the dread "suspension clause" of the standard actor's contract. That language allowed the studios to suspend without pay any actors who refuse a role assigned to them - and then tack the missed time onto the end of their contracts. It was a landmark decision that spelled the end of the once-mighty studio system.

Not that Bette was taking one for the team. "Mind you, I didn't fight it as a test case for the whole film industry," she told reporters at the time. "I fought it for myself and for my career."

Remarkably, she succeeded on that level, too. Even though she lost the case - and remained tethered to Warner Brothers - the publicity smashed once and for all the ridiculous series of images of Bette the studio had been trying to peddle: first the sweet sister, then the glamour queen. Now the world knew the real Bette - a tough, ornery woman who tells it like it is, and to hell with the consequences. And the public expected her to play such characters on the big screen.

This dynamic was not lost on Warner Brothers, which began considering her for more challenging, complex scripts. It also planned to hype Bette's explosive, difficult personality, with which it was intimately familiar. If Bette Davis wanted to be contentious, fine. They'd sell it. "In a way, my defeat was a victory," she said many years later. "At last we were seeing eye to eye on my career. I was aching to work and they were eager to encourage me."

When Bette arrived in New York, she found Ham busy working for Tommy Dorsey's band. They agreed he should stay and continue to try his luck there. By now, the marriage was clearly coming apart;

if Bette could survive her legal ordeal in London without him, there really wasn't much need for his companionship. Ham took Bette and Ruthie to the train station - and mother and daughter pulled into Hollywood in November of 1936.

When the press came calling, Bette took a humbler stance, telling reporters that she'd just have to put her head down and work harder than ever. Then she hand-delivered a personal letter to Jack Warner, saying she was ready to get back to work as soon as he had a job for her. Warner told her to report to the studio on Monday, November 23, to begin filming the crime drama, *Marked Woman.*

In this melodrama, based on real-life events, Bette would play Mary, identified as a nightclub "hostess" who stands up to a mob boss (due to the Hollywood censorship standards, they couldn't use the word prostitute). Bette liked the script and began to feel that she was finally being taken more seriously by her employers.

In the movie, Mary is called to testify against a gangster named Vanning but lies on the witness stand rather than face the wrath of the crime boss. After her sister is killed by Vanning's henchmen, she has a change of heart and squeals on the mob, which leads to a brutal beating from the gangster, leaving her disfigured.

Bette, of course, remained feisty on the set.

She was not, for instance, happy with the job the makeup artists did on her the day she was supposed to have been pummeled - she looked much too pretty. So after lunch, when she returned to the set, she stopped by the office of executive producer Hal Wallis sporting two black eyes, what appeared to be a broken nose, and gauze everywhere. Wallis laughed, then told her to take it down a notch. The broken nose was too much.

She still looked sufficiently awful for the scene, however, wearing a bandage on one cheek and gauze around her head, the black eyes and bruises completing the look. To further enhance her performance, she pinched her mouth in a way that revealed her emotional scars as well as the physical. It was not the kind of look Hollywood preferred for its leading ladies – but for this unsparing film, it worked spectacularly well.

After her role in *Marked Woman*, Bette's parts returned to the trite and traditional – a genre boxing film with Humphrey Bogart, *Kid Galahad,* and a drama with Henry Fonda, *That Certain Woman* – but she had fun with a farce co-starring Leslie Howard called *It's Love I'm After*. The movie's humor wasn't as sophisticated as she would have liked, but at least she got to wear dresses by the noted costume designer Orry-Kelly and have some laughs with Howard as a couple of egotistical entertainers who can't seem to make it to the altar.

That brought her batting average up to .500 for 1937 - two for four - a far more respectable showing than in years past - and she was beginning to enjoy life at Warner Brothers more and more.

As Bette focused on her work, her sister fell in love.

This could have been cause for celebration, given Bobby's struggles with mental illness, but Bette had trouble dealing with it: Though she was glad to be off the hook financially for Bobby, she was jealous. Why? Because her sister had never had to work - nor would she need to now. Also, Bobby's new beau was Robert Cole Pelgram, a handsome twenty-year-old aviator and socialite.

By then, Ham had returned to California, so he joined Bette, Bobby, and Pelgram on their drive to Tijuana for the ceremony, which took place on August 18, 1937 – coincidentally, the fifth anniversary of Bette's and Ham's vows.

Seeing Bobby's happiness while her own marriage was crumbling was difficult for Bette. She was not in love with Ham anymore, but her craving for the comforts of home was so strong she could not leave him.

Bobby's marriage also released Bette from being the sole breadwinner and center of the family's attentions. But Bette had enjoyed being the rich one in the family, giving her a measure of power over Bobby's and Ruth's lives. She was happy that her mother, who had sacrificed so much for her, was now living a life of luxury. But it bothered Bette that Ruthie seemed to take her generosity for granted and did not fully appreciate how hard she worked for that money.

"To Mother, Hollywood was a playground and movie actresses spent their days floating through an atmosphere of Chanel-scented flattery, adoration, and glamour," she said later. "I don't believe that Ruthie ever believed I worked once I arrived."

On that point, Ruthie was mistaken. Not only was Bette working harder than ever, churning out one movie after another, but she was struggling to make ends meet. In 1937, she asked Jack Warner for a $14,000 advance to pay her legal bills. Instead, Warner arranged for the Bank of America to set up a loan repayment program for Bette, with weekly installments coming out of her salary.

By ordinary standards, Bette was making an enormous amount of money – spent mostly on her family and legal bills – but it was hard not to be resentful when she saw how much other stars of her caliber were pulling down. A 1937 *Hollywood Citizen Examiner* article reported that Bette earned $53,200 that year [about $918,000 today] but Greta Garbo made nearly nine times as much, $472,499, while Irene Dunne earned a hefty $259,587, and Katharine Hepburn was paid $238,703.

With her salary locked in under her contract – and in no position to wage another court battle - Bette tried to play nice with the studio. But it was hard.

That summer, Warner Brothers cast her in the romantic musical comedy *Hollywood Hotel* opposite Dick Powell. The script called for her to play two roles - an irritable film star who drops out of sight when she doesn't get a part she wants, and a *doppelgänger* who takes her place for publicity purposes. It hit a little too close to home, and Bette flat-out refused. This time, Warner Brothers let it go and didn't force the issue.

Meanwhile, as she haggled with her bosses over her assignments, Bette was upset that she was not landing the dream job she had been coveting: Scarlett O'Hara in *Gone with the Wind*. According to Jack Warner, he could have purchased the screen rights to Margaret Mitchell's bestselling novel for $50,000, but unlike David O. Selznick, who ultimately produced the film, he wasn't willing to invest $5 million to make the movie. Warner conceded that the loss of the part was a major setback for Bette; had he made the movie, he certainly would have cast her as Scarlett.

"It could have been written for me," Bette moaned later. "I was as perfect for Scarlett as Clark Gable was for Rhett." However, Bette was hardly alone in feeling that way. During a famously agonizing search that lasted from 1936 to 1938, Selznick considered nearly every famous actress in America for the part – Tallulah Bankhead, Joan Crawford, Katharine Hepburn, and Lana Turner among others. Finally, he awarded it to the little-known British actress Vivien Leigh, who rode the role to an Academy Award for Best Actress and everlasting fame.

As the *Gone With The Wind* casting drama was consuming Hollywood, Bette was cheered up by getting a choice assignment from Warner Brothers – the spoiled and willful Julie Marsden in the romantic drama *Jezebel* – just the kind of bad-girl role she had been begging to do.

Finally, she had a part she could sink her teeth into. Thinking of Julie as "a blood sister of Scarlett's," Bette began plotting her portrayal of a woman who pushes the limits of propriety in New Orleans society by wearing a red dress to a southern society ball - a taboo for unmarried women, who were expected to wear white.

"Willful, perverse and proud, she was every inch the Southern belle," Bette recalled. "She had the same cast-iron fragility, the same resourcefulness, the same rebellion" as Scarlett O'Hara. In fact, Julie was the best part she had been given since Mildred in the celebrated film *Of Human Bondage*.

But then Warner Brothers announced that William Wyler had been hired to direct *Jezebel*. Bette was aghast. Years before, soon after arriving in

Hollywood, she had had a short and unpleasant encounter with the director. Her employer, Universal, told her to report to Wyler, who was directing a drama called *A House Divided*, and the wardrobe department insisted she wear a cotton dress that was too revealing in front. Embarrassed to wear it, she gamely rushed to the set anyway. Wyler glared at her and said to one of his assistants, "What do you think of these girls who show their chests and think they can get jobs?" Upset, Bette did not do well on the screen test, and the part was given to another actress.

Now that she was a big star, it was time for revenge. Bette arranged a meeting with Wyler, but it was hard to unleash her fury at him because he said he had no recollection of the incident. He also seemed mortified by her story. "He actually turned green," Bette recalled. "He was genuinely apologetic, saying he had come a long way since those days. I could not help but believe he was sincere."

From that moment on, Bette became one of Wyler's most ardent champions. "It was *he* who helped me realize my full potential as an actress," she said later. Having been nominated for his first Academy Award for *Dodsworth*, released the previous year, Wyler was at the beginning of a long winning streak of great films and would win Oscars for *Mrs. Miniver* (1942), *The Best Years of Our Lives* (1946), and *Ben-Hur* (1959).

But Wyler, whom she called a "handsomely homely dynamo," was also a legendary perfectionist who could make any actor's life a living hell. "Do you want me to put a chain around your neck?" he would scream at Bette. "Stop moving your head!"

Bette, also a perfectionist and workaholic, wasn't intimidated at all. Actually, she ate it up. Finally, she was in a high-budget film with a fabulous script, a great director, and an exceptional cast: Henry Fonda, George Brent, Donald Crisp, and Fay Bainter, who would win an Academy Award for Best Supporting Actress for *Jezebel.*

Bette knew the going would be tough in her very first scene, when Julie enters her house. To show her cavalier attitude, Wyler wanted her to lift her skirt with her riding crop. Bette tried it a dozen times, but he still wasn't satisfied. "He wanted a complete establishment of character with one gesture," Bette recalled. It took a draining forty-five takes, but he finally got what he wanted - or at least close enough.

With filming interrupted by Wyler's incessant demands for re-shoots - and Henry Fonda's need to return to New York for the birth of his daughter, Jane - Warner Brothers decided to remove Wyler as director. Furious, Bette intervened, threatening to quit the film unless Wyler stayed. The studio backed down, but only after she proposed working late each day to make up for the lost time. So she worked until midnight every night, arriving back on the set early the next morning.

Part of her devotion to Wyler was clearly artistic. "I had known all the horrors of no direction and bad direction," she said. "I now knew what a great director was and what he could mean to an actress."

But there was a deeply personal side to it as well: During the filming, Bette fell in love with him. With her husband in New York most of the time – Ham was now trying to make it as a talent agent – Bette and Wyler embarked on an affair that lasted throughout the filming of *Jezebel.*

In her two memoirs, Bette was highly selective about which affairs she mentioned and which she omitted. Wyler was among those left out, but during those glorious months, she appeared to have found an artistic soulmate – someone who was as exacting, precise, and bullheaded as she was. Late in life, she confessed to biographer Charlotte Chandler that Wyler "was the love of my life, in case you don't know." Making *Jezebel* with him, she said, was "the time in my life of my most perfect happiness."

But the film's exhausting shooting schedule and her affair with her demanding director took a toll on Bette. She was showing signs of depression. She suffered painful leg cramps on a day she was scheduled to perform a crucial dancing scene and contracted a severe cold and lingering bronchitis after filming in the rain. In one scene, when Bette's Julie was supposed to tap her cheeks with a hairbrush to bring out their color, she overdid it and wound up with bruises that took days to heal.

As 1937 came to a close, production on *Jezebel* was so far behind schedule that producers demanded the company work on New Year's Day. It was on that first day of 1938 that Bette was informed her father had died of a heart attack at his home in Belmont, Massachusetts. He was fifty-four.

But she did not attend his January 3 funeral at the Mt. Auburn Crematory Chapel in Cambridge, Massachusetts. Her excuse: She was busy filming the movie. But, in truth, their relationship was so badly broken that traveling across the country to pay her respects was simply not a high priority.

In February 1938, production for *Jezebel* ended. So did Bette's affair with Wyler. Later, she would say that she had been too afraid to pursue him after that. She could never be the kind of wife he wanted, she said - subservient and serene, the perfect hostess. Bette may have been flattering herself, however: Wyler seemed to have no interest in marrying her; he was the one who ended the relationship.

Coming down from the dizzying artistic and romantic high of *Jezebel*, Bette's nerves and health were in a frail state. Dr. Noyes advised the studio that she was not in any condition to make another picture. For once, Jack Warner listened and gave her a few months off.

*Jezebel* opened in March 1938 at Radio City Music Hall to generally good reviews and a strong box office: On a budget of $1.25 million, the film earned $1.5 million. Though some critics found the ending unconvincing - when Bette's character finds redemption - they raved about her performance. *Film Daily* called it "a really outstanding screen triumph for Bette Davis. She plays an emotional role that calls for running the gamut of emotions, and she handles the part with consummate artistry."

The following year, Bette was nominated for an Academy Award for Best Actress (as, ironically, was Margaret Sullavan, Wyler's ex-wife). *Jezebel* was nominated for Best Picture, but Bette was upset that both Wyler and Henry Fonda were snubbed since she considered their contributions so crucial to the film's success.

Wyler was one of Bette's eight escorts who accompanied her to the Academy Awards ceremony February 23, 1939, at the Biltmore Hotel. She was still stung by the scorn heaped upon her for the simple navy-and-white checked dress she wore to the ceremony three years earlier - and Joan Crawford's cutting remark. This time, she left nothing to chance. She went all out, choosing an elegant brown gown with a tight bodice and full, bouffant skirt.

And, to her surprise, she won again. When called to the stage by Sir Cedric Hardwicke, who presented the award, Bette took the opportunity to praise Wyler, insisting that he stand and be recognized for his brilliant direction.

This time, her Oscar was no consolation prize - she had truly earned it. Though she would be nominated eight more times, more than any other actress up to that point, it would be last time she actually took home a trophy. In retrospect, that made it a truly special moment. At age thirty, Bette was starting the most rewarding phase of her career - and she became box-office gold for Warner Brothers.

Although there would be challenges to come, of course - bad scripts, difficult directors, unreliable co-stars, and continuing health problems - Bette was on top of the world: "I was never surer of myself professionally than at this moment."

# 8

# "I SECURED MY CAREER AND MY STARDOM FOREVER."

Winning an Academy Award for *Jezebel* was part of a streak of good fortune that made the late 1930s one of the most successful periods of Bette's life. She would negotiate a more lucrative contract with Warner Brothers; make four hit films in a row in a single year (1939); earn her third Oscar nomination, for *Dark Victory*; attract the attention of the notorious Hollywood casanovas Errol Flynn and Howard Hughes; and fall in love with the man who would become her second husband.

But, as was typical of Bette Davis, none of these achievements occurred without a great deal of trauma, heartache, and professional rancor – not to mention a divorce from her childhood sweetheart, Ham.

For her, the hard way seemed to be the only way.

First up for Bette was money. After collecting her Oscar trophy in February, she scheduled a meeting with Jack Warner. Bette had come a long way since signing with him six years earlier, and she wanted to be paid for it. "I was," she said, "now a sovereign state demanding my own tithe - a member of the commonwealth. I had never been able to keep my mouth shut, but now mine was a voice that couldn't be ignored."

Bette knew that actresses have a short shelf life in Hollywood. At thirty years old, she was not sure how long studio bosses and audiences would continue to demand her talents - and wanted financial security for herself as well as her mother and sister. "No more peanuts!" she vowed. "No more haggling!" With *Jezebel* a runaway favorite, she told Warner bluntly, "I want my share."

Eager to keep Bette happy and fearful of losing her when her existing contract expired, Warner agreed to a new deal that – though it didn't give her everything she asked for - did give her enough of the pie to keep her happy. In retrospect, it was a smart move by the studio. Bette would stay with Warner Brothers for another eleven years and become its number-one box-office draw, regularly making the Quigley Poll of the top ten money-making stars based on votes from U.S. movie exhibitors.

During this period, though, Bette was still wrestling with bad scripts - and had not lost her penchant for confrontation. In 1938, the year before starting her new contract, the studio had assigned her the weepy melodrama *Comet Over Broadway*; she refused and was suspended. Then she was offered a Busby Berkeley comedy, *Garden of the Moon*, which she also refused, and was slapped with another suspension. Finally, she was offered a role she liked – Louise Elliott, a newlywed with a troubled husband in a drama called *The Sisters,* starring opposite Errol Flynn.

Famous for his swashbuckler roles, Flynn was a notoriously hard-drinking womanizer whose careless approach to acting was the antithesis of Bette's meticulous work ethic. He seemed to think of filmmaking as just another conquest, the cinematic equivalent of carving another notch in his belt. Later, Bette called him "handsome, arrogant, and utterly enchanting," qualities that made him perfectly suited for his part as a restless, confused sportswriter who abandons Bette's character.

Flynn was intrigued by his co-star. It seemed to drive him crazy that Bette did not throw herself at him, as most women did. One day, he smiled and said, "I'd love to proposition you, Bette, but I'm afraid you'd laugh at me."

"You're so right, Errol," she said dryly.

"He bit his lip, waved his arm through the air and bowed in mock chivalry like Captain Blood," Bette recalled later. "He was extremely graceful in retreat."

But there was another legendary ladies man Bette could not resist: The eccentric tycoon Howard Hughes. In her memoir, *A Lonely Life*, Bette was coy, as usual. She did not mention Hughes by name but was clearly referring to him when she described her "catastrophic relationship with the prototype of the Hollywood male. He was extremely attractive and one of the wealthiest men in the West - or East for that matter."

Charles Higham, in his biography, *Bette: The Life of Bette Davis*, confirms that Bette's affair with Hughes took place around the same time as his off-and-on relationship with Katharine Hepburn. Hughes sometimes suffered from impotence, according to Higham, which made Bette a suitable partner because she was not as beautiful as the other actresses he dallied with and was therefore less threatening. "She set his mind free of anxiety," Higham wrote. (Two of Bette's other biographers, Lawrence Quirk, author of *Fasten Your Seat Belts: The Passionate Life of Bette Davis*, and James Spada, who wrote *More Than a Woman: An Intimate Biography of Bette Davis*, delve more deeply into the relationship.)

Bette and Hughes met at a benefit at the Beverly Hills Hotel in September 1938, where Bette was selling raffle tickets for the Tailwaggers, an organization that rescued lost and abandoned dogs, a cause she was passionate about. Their relationship developed into an affair and Bette would visit Hughes's house on Malibu beach, where he reportedly covered his bed with gardenias before making love. The wacky mogul also liked to use his aviation skills to impress women he was interested in. With Hepburn, he landed his plane on a golf course as her group was playing, then took out his clubs and finished the round with them (he had to practically disassemble the plane to get it off the fairway). With Bette, Hughes "used to buzz my house in Manhattan Beach on his way to Russia or Afghanistan or you name it," she said.

The press was aware that Bette's marriage to Ham was strained, but not that she was having an affair with Hughes. In September of 1938, she admitted that she and Ham were having difficulties; soon afterward, gossip columnist Harrison Carroll reported that Ham had moved out of their Coldwater Canyon house, which Bette described as "a marriage vacation."

Looking back at her marriage later, Bette compared their home to a movie set - "a façade, a temporary scene for pointless arguments." Their scenes were played by childhood sweethearts who naively thought their union would never end.

On November 22, Ham filed for divorce, and it

was granted soon afterward. "She reads in bed," he testified, explaining his grounds. "She neglected me for her work."

Bette had to agree. "In the final analysis," she said later, "I guess this was the truth."

Among the difficult moments of their marriage was when Bette, at Ham's insistence, had two abortions – a fact she revealed to *Playboy* writer Bruce Williamson in 1982. "Being the dutiful wife, that's what I did," Bette said. "And I guess I will thank him all my life. Because if I'd had those two children . . . I see myself at fifty, with the children all grown up, wondering whether or not I ever would have made it. I think there's nothing sadder, and I'm sure I'd have given it all up if I'd had children earlier."

Though Bette knew the dissolution of her marriage was inevitable, she waxed nostalgic about it later. "My first real love was my first husband, Ham Nelson," she said. "There is no doubt about it, a girl's first exposure to sex is a powerful drug. Even after we were divorced, I still loved him and saw him often."

Now back on the singles' market, Bette knew finding love would not be easy. Later, she would poke fun at her situation, calling herself "Betteus Davisus, she wolf - habitat northeast coast of United States to southern clime of Pacific Ocean - noted for polygamous quest of perfect mate and ferocious independence. Belongs to no pack, condemned by duality to eternal solitude."

Fortunately, her job often required shooting passionate scenes with handsome men, providing a regular source of romance off the set. That was certainly the case with the first of her successful 1939 films, which Bette would later say was her all-time favorite – *Dark Victory*, based on the short-lived Broadway play of the same name starring Tallulah Bankhead. Bette had begged Jack Warner to purchase the rights to the play from David Selznick, who had originally intended to cast Greta Garbo and Fredric March, but could not because they were otherwise occupied with *Anna Karenina*.

No one at Warner Brothers was interested in *Dark Victory*, however, except for David Lewis, associate producer of *The Sisters*. Bette and Lewis teamed up and asked Edmund Goulding, who'd done the star-studded classic *Grand Hotel*, to direct the movie version of *Dark Victory*. He agreed. With Lewis and Goulding on her side, Bette was able to talk Warner into acquiring the rights, even if he wasn't completely sold on the idea. After all, it wasn't exactly uplifting material: Bette's character, Judith Traherne, is a socialite who is diagnosed with a terminal brain tumor.

"Who is going to want to see a picture about a girl who dies?" Warner said to Bette on the first day of shooting. "But it is a great part and I'm happy you are having a chance to play her."

The subject matter may have been grim, but shooting it made Bette happy because she got to appear opposite George Brent, who played the doctor who falls in love with Bette's Judith. Brent had by now divorced Ruth Chatterton, leaving him finally available. Having had strong feelings for him since their first film together six years earlier, Bette began an affair with Brent that would continue, on-and-off, for years.

"It was inevitable from our first meeting through the seven films we had made together, that we would one day have a romance," she said later, noting that the affection his Dr. Frederick Steele had for Bette's character seemed to spill over into real life. "The doctor's sympathy and love for Judith, plus her dependence on him, influenced, I think, both of us."

Nevertheless, it was a difficult shoot. Bette was emotionally drained from the stress of her divorce and also physically ill. Within a week, she felt so miserable that she asked producer Hal Wallis to let her drop the part and give it to someone else. Wallis refused, telling Bette that her condition could only enhance the film. "I've seen the rushes," he told her, "Stay sick!"

Everyone involved with the picture knew Bette was on the verge of collapse, and she did little to mask her anxiety. After six weeks in production, in late November, Bette took three sick days. When she came back, the scene in which Judith realizes she's going blind was especially difficult. A production manager said she cried so hysterically that she barely got through the scene. Bette knew she wasn't being true to her character – Judith was not the self-pitying type – and that upset her even further.

In the film's final scene, in which Judith Traherne pulls herself onto her bed and tells her maid she does not wish to be disturbed, Bette's exhaustion worked to her advantage - she looked close enough to death to easily portray a dying woman.

When *Dark Victory* was released in April, it was a blockbuster, ranking as one of the highest-grossing films of the year, and drew positive reviews like the one from *Variety* that called Bette's performance "powerful and impressive." At the Academy Awards the following year, Bette was nominated for Best Actress for *Dark Victory*, but, as expected, lost to Vivian Leigh's Scarlett O'Hara in *Gone with the Wind.*

Even in losing the Oscar, Bette could not get a break. On the night of the awards ceremony, she was so exhausted from working all day on her next film, *Juarez*, that she decided to go home after dinner, before the award presentations. "Bette! Are you mad?" Ruthie cried. "Everyone will think you are a bad loser!" So Bette grudgingly stayed until two o'clock in the morning, applauded her rival's victory, and then went home. That didn't stop the gossip mongers from whispering, "Did you see Davis leave in a huff when she lost? . . . Davis walked out in a rage!" She realized she should have followed her original instinct and not give a damn what people thought.

In all other respects, *Dark Victory* was an enormous hit that was immediately followed by three more winners –

*Juarez*, *The Old Maid*, and *The Private Lives of Elizabeth and Essex*.

"In the year 1939, I secured my career and my stardom forever," she said later.

(In fact, her hot hand continued the following year, when both movies she made – *All This and Heaven Too* and *The Letter* – were also audience favorites. Astonishingly, Bette received five Academy Award nominations in a row from 1938 to 1942, a record that has never been surpassed. Greer Garson tied it with five straight between 1942 and 1946.)

After filming for *Dark Victory* wrapped on December 5, 1938, Bette had only a week off before sweeping right into her next hit film, the historical drama *Juarez*, that showed how sophisticated Bette's acting had become. Two years in the making, *Juarez* is an epic tale about Mexico's fight for independence from Napoleon's rule that centers on Benito Juarez (Paul Muni), who rises from poverty to serve as Mexico's first president. Bette played Carlotta, the wife of Maximilian, Napoleon's puppet ruler of Mexico. The making of the movie was an epic adventure in itself. When she stepped onto the set for the first time, wearing a $2,500 wig made with hair from fourteen women, production had already been underway for nearly two months.

During the movie, Carlotta goes mad, and Bette got the point across with her formidable technique – acting nervous, paranoid or pretending to be catatonic, each dramatic change accentuated by special makeup and shooting through a filtered lens. When the distressed Carlota bursts in on Louis Napoleon (played by Claude Rains), a scarf falling from Carlota's hat demonstrates that she's losing her mind as she screams, "What else might a Hapsburg have expected from a bourgeois Bonaparte!"

As accomplished as she was getting, Bette retained her capacity to be awed by more seasoned actors. *Juarez* marked the first time Bette got to work with Claude Rains, later known for his iconic roles in *Casablanca* and *Lawrence of Arabia*. She was surprised to find that she literally quaked with fear in Rains's presence.

"When he looked at me during our scene as Napoleon would look at Carlotta, with loathing, I thought he, Claude Rains, held loathing of me, Bette Davis, as a performer!" she said later. "We have laughed about it many times since."

That didn't mean she got along with everyone. Quite the contrary. With her growing acclaim, Bette knew she could get away with a great deal of misbehavior – and she did. "I will never deny that I was on occasion insufferably rude and ill-mannered in the cultivation and preservation of my career," she said. "I had no time for pleasantries."

In her next film, *The Old Maid*, teamed up again with director Edmund Goulding and her sometimes-lover George Brent, she was just as volatile on the set. An adaptation of the Pulitzer-Prize winning play by Zoë Akins and Edith Wharton's novella, the film marked the first time Bette had to share equal screen time with a female co-star: Miriam Hopkins played the sister who raises the illegitimate child of Bette's character, who becomes "Aunt" Charlotte.

It did not go well. "I was never mad about the part," Bette said later, but she had originally wanted to play both sisters. Instead, the more colorful role went to Hopkins, who had worked with Bette in Rochester, New York years earlier when both were part of George Cukor's stock company. Back then, Hopkins was the star and Bette the unknown ingénue. Now Bette's star was ascending, and Hopkins felt threatened. Hopkins resented Bette for her Academy Award for *Jezebel*, a role Hopkins had originated on Broadway. She was also upset about rumors that Bette had had an affair with her husband Anatole Litvak when he directed Bette in *The Sisters* (the romance was widely believed to be a short one, though Bette never confessed to it).

Bette knew trouble was brewing when Hopkins showed up on the set wearing a replica of one of Bette's costumes from *Jezebel.* Later, Hopkins altered her makeup to make her look younger than Bette during a scene in which they both were supposed to be older. Both actresses called in sick at various times, causing production to fall behind schedule.

"It was obvious she wanted me to blow my stack," Bette recalled. She kept her temper – at least on the set: "I went home every night and screamed at everybody."

Bette had the last laugh, however. In his review in *The New York Times,* Frank S. Nugent wrote that "Miss Davis has given a poignant and wise performance, hard and austere of surface, yet communicating through it the deep tenderness, the hidden anguish of the heart-broken mother." Hopkins, meanwhile, turned in "a less certain characterization . . . [of] the malignance lurking beneath a charming manner."

For so many of Bette's movies, the drama on the set was more gripping than the film itself. This was true of her next film as well, another costume drama called *The Private Lives of Elizabeth and Essex,* about the relationship between Queen

Elizabeth I (Bette) and Robert Devereux, the Earl of Essex (Errol Flynn). The entire production was a fiasco, with one bitter argument after another, fraying nerves and stirring resentment.

One problem was Flynn. Bette was displeased at his casting. "He wasn't an experienced enough actor to cope with the complicated blank verse the play had been written in," she said later, but the studio refused to hire her first choice, Laurence Olivier, because he wasn't nearly as well-known as Flynn at that time. Halfway through production, Flynn crashed his car while driving drunk and was left with scars all over his face. In one scene, when Bette as Elizabeth slaps Essex across the face, Bette - her hand full of jewelry - smacked Flynn so hard he never forgave her.

Even selecting the title of the picture - which would determine who got top billing - was a matter of contention. Warner Brothers wanted Flynn at the top of the marquee and suggested the movie be called *The Knight and the Lady*, making it a "man's picture." Bette would have none of it - if it became a man's picture, she told Jack Warner, she wouldn't make it at all, even if her name got top billing. In May of 1939, her final day of filming for *The Old Maid*, Warner informed her she would indeed get top billing in the new film, but a new title had yet to be agreed upon.

Later, Warner Brothers proposed the title be changed to *The Lady and the Knight*. Bette still was not happy and wrote Jack Warner that the issue was upsetting her so that she would have difficulty finishing the film unless it was changed. It was.

During the making of *The Private Lives of Elizabeth and Essex,* Bette got some advice she never forgot, a perspective that deeply influenced her approach to choosing roles. When filming began, she was terribly unsure whether, having just turned thirty-one, she could play a sixty-year-old queen. When she expressed her concern to the great actor Charles Laughton, who had won an Oscar for playing King Henry VIII, he said, "Never stop daring to hang yourself, Bette!" From that day on, Bette vowed she would never stop taking big chances with film roles; despite the risks, it was the only way to grow as an actress.

Though *Elizabeth and Essex* had its good points - Bette's multi-layered performance, Orry-Kelly's queenly gowns, and a magnificent score by Erich Wolfgang Korngold - the movie was, at best, mediocre. Betty was particularly unhappy with Flynn's Essex, but admitted years later that she had been wrong; he was actually pretty good. The film was also tremendously profitable, earning $550,000 ($9.5 million today).

When shooting was over, Bette desperately needed to rest. After making four films in rapid succession, she was near the breaking point. Her romance with Brent was going nowhere. Longing for her roots, she went back to New England, to her old haunts – to Newton and Boston in Massachusetts, and to Ogunquit and Ocean Park in Maine. In each place, everything felt exactly the same and yet totally different. Perversely, going home made her feel more homesick than ever.

As the summer of 1939 melted into fall, she sat for days watching the waves pound the rocky Maine coast. The irony was inescapable. Awards were pouring in from all over the world, and she was named one of the world's outstanding women, along with Eleanor Roosevelt, by the *American Dictionary*. Her movies were so profitable that the press began calling her "The Fourth Warner Brother." After years of being derided for her looks, she could now say, "I brought more people into theatres than all the sexpots put together."

And yet Bette had never been more miserable in her life. Her marriage had been an abject failure. She loved being independent, free to do as she pleased – and cherished her reputation as a strong woman who took no guff from anyone – but was simultaneously terribly lonely, adrift, needy. "I hate this life I've been thrown into," she thought. "I don't want to end up alone at fifty - unsafe, desperate, pitiable - without someone who needs me."

Deeply unhappy as she was, she could not bring herself to return to Hollywood. So Bette headed up to New Hampshire's white mountains and, as the leaves turned gold and red, checked into

Peckett's-on-Sugar-Hill Inn, a playground for the wealthy known for its world-class ski school.

There she met Arthur Farnsworth, the assistant manager of the inn. Farney, as she would call him, was a charming man of thirty-three from a New England blue-blood family. Handsome, educated, and divorced, he was also an aeronautic engineer, experienced pilot, and violinist. Suddenly, Bette was not so lonely anymore. In her mountain retreat, thanks to Farney, she began to feel at home again. In fact, she loved the place so much that she would later buy 150 acres of rolling land there and make Sugar Hill her haven from the stress and superficiality of Tinseltown.

"It was here that I came out of my blue funk - here that I felt happy for the first time in years," she said later. "New Hampshire and Farney were a tonic for me."

With her career secure and her fame growing, meeting Farney gave Bette a glimpse of what a fully rounded life might look like, brimming with professional and personal contentment. As the weather grew colder, she kept finding excuses to extend her vacation and stay close to her new boyfriend. It was almost as if she sensed that once she returned to Hollywood, and her stormy career, reality would bring her back to earth.

And so it did.

# 9
# "CREATION IS HELL!"

When Bette finally returned to California from her idyllic vacation in New Hampshire, her life was essentially the same - only more amplified by her increasing fame. Yes, she had found in those White Mountains a man and a place that warmed her heart. And both would continue to offer her some temporary comfort when she could get away from Hollywood.

But she was still the same old Bette, who would continue to find conflict wherever she turned, from the bedroom to the soundstage. She would have romantic adventures that would lead to clashes among competing suitors before finally deciding to marry Farney, who was - if not quite Mr. Right - Mr. Good Enough. And she would make more money for Warner Brothers, and herself, with hit movies that somehow survived the agonizing process of making them.

Meanwhile, her family provided a reliable source of angst. While Bette was in New Hampshire, her sister gave birth to her first child, a girl named Fay, back in Los Angeles. But the joyous occasion was soon eclipsed by trauma, as Bobby had another nervous breakdown. "I never forgave myself for not going to California to be with her," Bette said later. "My guilt became a deadweight."

Finally, in early 1940, Bette fled the New Hampshire winter and returned to sunny Los Angeles. With Bobby incapacitated by her mental illness, infant Fay and her father, Bob Pelgram, stayed with Bette until Bobby could get well again.

Though Bette liked to complain about the fast-track Hollywood lifestyle and yearned for the simplicity of rural New England, she clearly seemed to enjoy the celebrity whirlwind that swept her up as soon as she returned to the West Coast. In fact, readers of the gossip columns got whiplash trying to keep up with Bette's romantic life during that spring of 1940.

In March, the press reported that her beau, Arthur Farnsworth, and his sister were staying with her, and there might be a wedding in the near future. But gossip columnist Louella Parsons had a different take: She had a feeling Bette would marry again, but it wouldn't be Farnsworth. Parsons disclosed that Bette had a new love interest, a man from the Warner Brothers publicity department. In April, Bette sailed to Hawaii for a ten-day vacation with her friend Robin Brown, and they were joined by the man Parsons was referring to – the studio's publicity director, Robert Taplinger.

With that, the gossip media went into overdrive. Dorothy Kilgallen wrote on May 6 that Warner Brothers was horrified by the Taplinger affair, but couldn't do anything, and when Bette was asked about it, she just giggled. On May 8, Jimmie Fidler reported that an upset Farnsworth was calling Bette in Hawaii to find out if the rumors were true. When she returned to California on May 13, Bette firmly denied reports that she was planning to get married to anyone.

In her memoirs, Bette mentions Taplinger just once, in a short aside when she called him "my loyal friend for thirty-five years, until his death from cancer at sixty." But at the end of May 1940, she was seen out and about town with him; in late June, writer Sidney Skolsky reported that Bette was receiving a gardenia daily on the set of the film she was making, *The Letter.* Everyone working on the movie was sure the flowers were from Taplinger.

As Bette's two boyfriends tried to figure out who was in and who was out, her career continued to skyrocket. In July, Bette's latest film, *All This and Heaven Too*, was released. It was Warner Brothers' $2.5 million response to Selznick's *Gone with the Wind*. The story is based on Rachel Field's novel about her real-life aunt whose scandalous love affair with a French nobleman in the mid-nineteenth century leads to the fall of France's King Louis-Philippe.

*All This and Heaven, Too* premiered at Hollywood's famous Carthay Circle Theatre before a crowd of some 15,000 people. As she greeted well-wishers, Bette felt like a queen and giggled privately with Ruthie about how far they had come since arriving in California ten years earlier. "No more of the indignities of impoverished anonymity," she said later.

The film was a critical and commercial success. *Variety* called it "film theater at its best," and *Film Daily* pronounced it "dramatically powerful, beautifully mounted and superbly cast." Ticket sales were so strong that it became Bette's most financially successful film so far.

When the premiere was over, Bette went back to work on her next film, *The Letter*, which starts off with a dramatic scene that further endeared her to critics and fans alike: A man staggers out the door of a colonial bungalow and onto the porch. Bette, wielding a gun, follows the man and shoots him five times. Then she lets the gun drop while she stares unmercifully at her kill. Based on a play by Somerset

Maugham, *The Letter* follows the story of Bette's character, Leslie Crosbie, who claims she killed the man only because he was drunk and trying to rape her. But soon, holes appear in her story.

Bette was ecstatic when her old flame, William Wyler was hired to direct. She would later describe him as a male version of herself, a severe taskmaster who insisted on having things his way – and she loved him for it.

What Bette could never abide was a happy, loving work environment where everybody agrees on everything – a sure prescription for a bad film, she said. Working with Wyler, whom she called a "tyrant," gave her a worthy opponent in the inevitable creative battles of the filmmaking process. "When working, Willie - like me - could be asked 'Whom do you hate today?'" Bette said later. "There is always something to fight in this most imperfect of worlds. Creation is hell!"

The battles paid off: Her performance in *The Letter* would earn Bette an Oscar nomination for the third straight year, and *The Hollywood Reporter* called it "one of the best pictures of the year."

Exhausted by her production schedule, Bette went back East for three months of rest when *The Letter* wrapped in July of 1940. But when the work was over, she had to face the demands of being a star: Nearly 1,000 fans were waiting when she got off the train at Boston's South Station; the *Boston Traveler* described the mob as "unruly autograph seekers and hero-worshippers, mostly young girls." Ten police officers escorted her through the crowd to a car that took her to her hotel, the swanky Ritz Carlton.

By that time, her romance with Taplinger was over and Farney was her steady. The passion level was not high, she admitted, but he was good enough. He respected her work and was proud of her - and since his life was far removed from the Hollywood scene, he had no interest in competing with her. Unlike Ham, he did not care how much money she made.

"I was not violently in love with Farney," she said later. "I loved his loving me, and our mutual love of the New England way of life was the tie that finally bound. . . . He was companionable, attractive, and a divine host. Plus, he was the most beautifully mannered man I've ever known."

Still not sold on him as a permanent mate, Bette rebuffed his repeated marriage proposals. Ruthie herself was on the fence about Farney. She was happy to have her daughter back after her divorce from Ham, but she didn't want to lose her again to another man. Still, she could not strenuously object to Farney, who was such an agreeable person. "He would someday inherit money, he was from a good family - important to Yankee mothers," Bette said. "I really think Ruthie found it hard not to like him."

That summer, Bette oversaw the renovation of her house in New Hampshire, which she called Butternut, after the swath of land in Sugar Hill where it was located. When finished, the living room had a white couch and red brick fireplace; the sizable kitchen had wooden cabinets painted white; the dining room had wallpaper with a scene featuring a boy who looked like Huckleberry Finn. In Bette's bedroom was a fireplace suspended from the ceiling with girders. The house also had servants' quarters and a large screened-in porch. With the closest neighbor about a quarter mile away, Bette was in heaven.

But Hollywood was calling, and Bette knew that a star's time in the limelight can be short and she must take full advantage when the iron is hot. In the fall, she returned to California, joined by Farney and his sister Barbara. When Warner Brothers assigned her to play Maggie Patterson, the wealthy but dull sweetheart of a multi-millionaire pilot in *The Great Lie*, she was not enthusiastic. But she finally agreed because fans had been pestering her to play a nice character for a change. The more interesting character, a fiery pianist named Sandra Kovak who is also in love with the pilot, went to Mary Astor.

Normally, this would have set off a nasty fight between Bette and a rival actress. And it seemed to start off that way. Astor, in her memoirs, said that Bette seemed sulky and remote on the set, chain smoking and idly swinging her foot. But Bette saw a kindred soul in Astor and opted for a more cooperative approach. After a few days, she called Astor into her dressing room and railed about how dissatisfied she was with the film. It was going to be awful, she said, unless they conspired to "rewrite this piece of junk to make it more interesting." What the film needed was some spice, and Bette wanted Astor's character to supply it, even though it meant Mary would get to have all the fun.

"Bette and I [became] as simpatico as a pair of dancers as we worked out the story," Astor recalled. People remarked that she stole the film out from under Bette - Astor would win the Academy Award for Best Supporting Actress - but, in fact, it was a rare case of Bette wrapping it up with a bow and handing it to her.

The new and improved Bette seemed to be entering a more stable phase in her life. She bought her first California home, a Tudor-style house in Glendale, on the bank of the Los Angeles River, which she named Riverbottom. And as 1940 came to a close, Bette made another big life decision: She finally gave in to Farney and agreed to marry him. True, he was not the love of her life but her most passionate romances - like the one with Wyler - were so explosive they could not possibly last. Bette decided that Farney was someone she could at least get along with – and possibly even be happy with. So why not give it a try?

On New Year's Eve, they tied the knot at a ranch in Rimrock, Arizona owned by Bette's friend Jane Bryan. The wedding entourage included Ruthie; Bette's hairdresser Margaret Donovan and her boyfriend, the makeup artist Perc Westmore; Bette's cousin John Favor; and Bette's dog Tibby. Bobby, feeling better now, flew in from Los Angeles with her husband.

It was all pretty quick as weddings of the rich and famous go: The newlyweds didn't go on a honeymoon because Bette was expected back at the studio for her next film, a slapstick comedy with James Cagney called *The Bride Came C.O.D.*

"Farney and I were happy," Bette said. "Our light was a low one but steady. He didn't have an ounce of jealousy. He never questioned me about anything I did. He let me run my own life."

She completed *The Bride Came C.O.D.* – so unfunny, Bette said later, she and Cagney "both reached bottom with this one." Afterward, she shared her love of New Hampshire, and her new husband, with the world on April 5, 1941 - her thirty-third birthday - when Warner Brothers agreed to premiere *The Great Lie* in Littleton, New Hampshire. (Not far from Franconia.)

As part of the event, the studio placed street signs with a Bette Davis theme all over town. For example, the All Saints Episcopal Church sat at the corner of *Dangerous* and *Dark Victory* streets. According to *The New York Times*, "Crowds of celebrities and curious swelled this quiet community five times its normal size of 4,500." The governors of New Hampshire and Vermont were there, and *Life* magazine did a four-page spread on the event. A prescreening stage show featured a 200-pound birthday cake made of plaster that was lowered onto the stage with cables; the actual, edible birthday cake weighed a staggering 103 pounds.

From that joyous occasion, it was back to the grueling maelstrom of movie-making – and it soon became clear that any suggestion of marriage, home ownership, and career stability mellowing Bette Davis was wishful thinking. Her next film, *The Little Foxes*, brought with it two signs of trouble: It would be directed by her ex-lover, William Wyler, and it came with a distinguished pedigree that put enormous pressure on Bette, triggering more fireworks.

*The Little Foxes* was based on the Lillian Hellman play of the same name about a wealthy family living in the South in the early 1900s. The original stage production, which ran for nearly a year on Broadway, starred Tallulah Bankhead in a highly acclaimed turn as Regina Giddens - a vicious money-grubber who plots to wrest control of her brothers' new cotton mill. The role was perfect for

Tallulah but seemed to suit Bette, too.

The previous summer, word had gotten around Hollywood that Sam Goldwyn had the movie rights and wanted to borrow Bette from Warner Brothers to play Regina. Wyler had insisted that Bette be hired over Bankhead, and Goldwyn agreed since none of Bankhead's films had been very successful at the box office. But Bette was hesitant, knowing that Bankhead seemed to own the role. "I begged the producer, Samuel Goldwyn, to let Tallulah Bankhead play Regina [but] he wouldn't let her," Bette said later.

To borrow Bette, Goldwyn and Warner Brothers came up with a complex deal that studio chief Jack Warner accepted partly because he owed Goldwyn $425,000 in gambling debts. Goldwyn would lend Gary Cooper to Warner Brothers to make *Sergeant York* in exchange for Bette for *The Little Foxes*. Under her contract, Bette was earning $3,000 a week, but when she discovered that Warner was receiving $385,000 from Goldwyn as part of the deal, she demanded, and ultimately received, a share of that payment as well. It was deeply satisfying for Bette to see Goldwyn spending so much for her – "the same Sam Goldwyn who, ten years before, had wailed at the sight of my test," she gloated, "and refused to hire me at three hundred a week."

But as usual, nothing, for Bette, came easily. She repeatedly clashed with Wyler about how to play Regina Giddens and struggled to make the character her own. She hadn't seen Bankhead play the part on Broadway and didn't particularly want to – not wanting to let it affect her interpretation of the character – but Goldwyn insisted. So, on their way from New Hampshire to California, Bette and Farney made a detour to Cleveland to see Bankhead's touring performance.

In Bankhead's hands, Regina was an icy, money-obsessed snake, but Wyler wanted Bette to play her a little more likable and less vile. Goldwyn and Wyler agreed that such a toxic female would prevent the movie from becoming a box office success. Bette thought the producer and director were simply afraid of this character - a woman so cruel that she watches her husband suffer a heart attack without handing him the medicine he needs.

By now, Bette was fed up with softening vicious female characters to appease less sophisticated movie-goers – not to mention the chauvinistic men who ran the movie business. She wanted Regina to be a bitch. "I insisted that Tallulah had played it the only way it could be played," Bette said later. In fact, she added, "Miss Hellman's Regina was written with such definition that it could only be played one way." But Wyler had other ideas, telling her to play Regina as a charming, poised, witty devil.

The disagreements on set between Bette and Wyler were constant, no doubt fueled by the bitterness of their failed love affair (by now, Wyler was married to the actress Margaret Tallichet). The fights started early, during makeup and wardrobe tests, with Bette getting what she felt was contradictory advice from Wyler and others, leaving her feeling insecure. Bette had asked her friend Perc Westmore to come to Goldwyn to do her makeup; one day, when she was made up with zinc oxide and water to get closer to the older age of her character, the blunt-talking Wyler upset her by cracking that she looked like a clown.

After constant criticism and changes to her wardrobe and makeup, Bette became more and more distraught, until finally, she was physically ill. A heat wave that sent temperatures on the set soaring above 100 degrees did not help matters. According to her attorney Dudley Furse, Bette decided she should leave the lot, and Goldwyn agreed to give her three weeks off. The press was aflutter, spreading rumors of her being pregnant, getting a divorce, fighting with Wyler and Goldwyn, or getting replaced by Miriam Hopkins or Katharine Hepburn. Others saw her absence as a ploy, though Bette herself never admitted as much. "It's a sit-down strike, not a nervous collapse," Erskine Johnson wrote in the *Los Angeles News*.

*The New York Times*'s Douglas Churchill noted that "The[se] outbursts were little different from those that marked the filming of *Jezebel*." In that film,

Bette would give in to the headstrong director. Now she challenged him at every turn. There were other pressures as well: Bette was working with a different studio, and a lot of money was at stake. Overwhelmed, she would see several doctors and require assurance from her director and producer that things would go smoother before she was able to step back on the set.

Visiting the set of the *Little Foxes* during the third week of June, Thomas Brady of *The New York Times* observed: "Miss Davis seemed intent last week on interpreting her role with gayety and daring; Wyler wanted subtle repression . . . Miss Davis was icy in deferring to his wishes, and each was monstrously patient with the other. When one scene reached its eighth or ninth take, Mr. Wyler told Miss Davis she was rattling off her lines. Her response was cool enough to make the set suitable for a Sonja Henie skating spectacle."

Battling every inch of the way, Bette and Wyler finally managed to finish the film. In August of 1941, *The Little Foxes* premiered at the 6,000-seat Radio City Music Hall in New York City and was seen by a total of 22,163 people on opening day, setting an all-time attendance mark. The film was also critically admired, being nominated for nine Academy Awards, including Bette for Best Actress, her fourth straight nomination.

But Bette was not satisfied, convinced that she

had given "one of the worst performances of my life." This was painful to admit because she still desperately wanted to please Wyler – despite their fights, she always held him in the highest regard as a director – and she knew Regina was a great role that had been played beautifully by Bankhead on stage. Though the film was highly praised, some critics said Bankhead's portrayal of Regina was better. By then, Wyler and Bette were so fed up with each other that they never worked together again.

At least Bette had a rare interlude of domestic happiness to fall back on. She and Farney returned to New Hampshire to rest and work on their house. It was the little white cottage she had always dreamed of, with a lawn and a barn, and surrounded by woods and flowers. Ruthie was deeply involved, too, planting birch trees and rose bushes. "It had all the peace of the English country homes I had adored so much," she said later. "I was again safely ensconced in a picture book life of respectable marriage."

But whenever Bette was happy, it seemed, Bobby was not. During this time, she was going through a divorce from Bob Pelgram and fighting for custody of their daughter. What led to the divorce is unclear because neither Bobby nor Bette discussed the details publicly. But without question, both sisters – and their mother – would continue to struggle to find any semblance of matrimonial bliss as the specter of the girls' absent father, Harlow Davis, continued to hang ominously over the family.

Sometimes, it seemed that bad luck followed both Davis sisters and their men. In October of 1941 – after Bette had finished making *The Man Who Came to Dinner* (another artistic and box-office hit) - Farney came down with a severe case of lobar pneumonia after flying to Minnesota to share some of his aviation expertise with a local businessman. It was his second bout of pneumonia that year. On October 20, he was admitted to a hospital in Minneapolis with a fever of 106.

The news reached Bette at the Los Angeles studio where she was filming *In This Our Life* with Olivia de Havilland. Because of fog and storms, it took her two days to get to Minneapolis by way of Kansas City, Des Moines, and Rochester, Minnesota. Farney was in critical condition when she arrived but was starting to show signs of improvement. Warner, unmoved by the emergency, cabled Bette immediately, demanding that she return to the film. Between this pressure and worrying about her husband, Bette became ill, too.

As she prepared to fly back to California, Farney's doctor insisted that she take the train instead, to protect her from the rigors of flying in the cold, loud, unpressurized airplanes of the early 1940s. Dr. J. C. Davis of Minneapolis sent a wire to Warner Brothers explaining that Bette had become so depleted that she needed four days to recuperate. She traveled back to Hollywood on the Super Chief, arriving on October 30, then headed straight to the set.

Bette's absence had put the film behind schedule, and by mid-December, Warner was furious. Tensions escalated further when Bette argued with producers about how to play her character and demanded continuous changes to her hair, makeup, and costumes. As her husband got better, eventually making a full recovery, Bette got sick, coming down with the flu.

Chaos was erupting outside the studio, too. On December 7, 1941, the Japanese attacked Pearl Harbor, dragging the United States into World War II. Three days later, director John Huston abruptly left the production of *In This Our Life* to take an assignment with the War Department. Raoul Walsh finished the film, but not before he and Bette clashed repeatedly. She refused to obey his directions and would not reshoot scenes that were already in the can, causing him to threaten to quit. Bette also contracted laryngitis, on top of everything else, halting shooting for several days.

Because of the delays, the film was not done until mid-January 1942, well over schedule. It was hardly the first time this had happened to a Bette Davis film - which Warner's head of production

Hal Wallis pointedly reminded her. Just as unpleasant to Wallis were the comment cards the studio received after a February preview of *In This Our Life*. Viewers did not like Bette's hair, makeup, and wardrobe - all changes she insisted upon - and Wallis laid into Perc Westmore for altering her look without permission.

In *The New York Times*, Bosley Crowther was also not impressed with her performance, writing, "She is forever squirming and pacing and grabbing the back of her neck. It is likewise very hard to see her as the sort of sultry dame that good men can't resist. In short, her evil is so theatrical and so completely inexplicable that her eventual demise in an auto accident is the happiest moment in the film. That, indeed, is what probably provoked the audience to cheer."

It was hard to imagine Bette's life becoming more chaotic, but that's exactly what happened in November of 1941.

During the constant crisis of making *In This Our life* and dealing with Farney's illness, she became the first actress to be named president of the Academy of Motion Picture Arts and Sciences.

Bette certainly did not need another film-industry battlefield full of landmines to wander into. But someone forgot to tell that to Darryl Zanuck of 20th Century Fox, who sponsored her candidacy. At first, it seemed like a harmless gesture on his part. After all, the position was largely ceremonial, a nod to her skyrocketing fame and box-office success. But Bette did not realize that. She mistakenly thought that, as president, she could really change things.

It wasn't that her ideas for the Academy were bad. In fact, they were eerily prescient. At a time of austerity, with the nation at war, she proposed that the Oscar ceremony do away with its ostentatious dinner-and-dancing event and suggested it be held in a theater instead. She also wanted to charge a $25 attendance fee and give the proceeds to war relief efforts. "The members of the board were horrified," she recalled later. "Such an evening would rob the Academy of all dignity."

For an actress with a reputation for selfishness, it was surprising for industry insiders to see this side of her – the Bette Davis who believes in grand causes, patriotism, and giving back. She also wanted to clean up the Oscar voting process that had famously denied her the Best Actress award for *Of Human Bondage* years earlier. So she proposed that extras on films not be allowed to cast ballots – partly because their votes often favored whichever studio hired them around the time of the voting.

"A pall fell on the room," she recalled, as she laid out her agenda. Walter Wanger, the previous president, demanded to know what she had against the Academy. The tension was so great, and

Bette's manner so abrasive, that she submitted her resignation a few days later. She had lasted all of two months. Zanuck had warned her that if she resigned, she would never work in Hollywood again. But she ignored him - and Zanuck refused to speak to Bette for nine years.

Later, Bette took some satisfaction in noting that within a few years, the Academy enacted both of her ideas – taking the vote away from extras and eliminating the dinner. The Oscars have been held in theaters ever since.

Her bruising fights with the Academy were hardly out of character for Bette. In fact, she was just getting warmed up. In the coming years, she would continue to clash with family, friends, lovers, directors, producers, fellow actors, reporters, fans, and just about anyone else she came into contact with. What kept her popular, however, was how refreshingly candid she was about her own flaws. "I have reached the conclusion," she wrote in an article for *Ladies Home Journal*, "that probably I am a very disagreeable person."

It was a revealing comment. One of the secrets to her success was portraying disagreeable people on screen in a way that won over the audience. But, as Bette was learning, the same qualities that create great art can also cause tremendous misery in real life.

Just ask any of her four husbands, especially Farney. He fought constantly with Bette and – perhaps as a result – soon met an untimely death.

# 10

# "IT WAS UNBELIEVABLE THAT HE WAS GONE - JUST LIKE THAT."

The decade of the 1940s began as war clouds gathered steadily, then finally exploded with the dropping of bombs by Japanese fighter planes attacking Pearl Harbor on December 7, 1941. From that moment on, nothing in America was the same. Like many other movie stars, Bette did whatever she could to help, including touring the country to encourage citizens to buy war bonds. Volunteering for a program called "Stars Over America," a joint effort between the U.S. Treasury Department and the film industry, Bette spoke at Rotary meetings, at rallies in auditoriums, and at gatherings in private homes throughout Iowa, Illinois, Missouri, Oklahoma, and Kansas.

At such events, Bette was her usual provocative

self. "Anyone who doesn't do what he can even if it's (donating) a twenty-five-cent stamp is not an American!" she thundered to a group of factory workers in Oklahoma City. When urged to be more subtle, she replied brusquely that someone needed to light a fire under people's rear ends.

She was, if nothing else, effective.

In St. Joseph, Illinois, she raised $177,000 ($2.8 million today) - nearly half of it in the first ten minutes. In Kansas City, she pulled in $650,000. In Tulsa, she stopped at a Douglas Aircraft factory to sell a portrait of herself as Julie Marsden in *Jezebel* for $250,000. Later that day, she spoke at Skelly Stadium and sold an autograph for $50,000. But Bette paid a price, too. Her travel schedule was so demanding that she came down with a cold bad enough to land her in a hospital.

All that, however, wasn't enough - for Bette, anyway. Sitting with the actor John Garfield in the Warner Brothers commissary, they decided to establish a Hollywood version of New York's famous Stage Door Canteen. Thousands of soldiers came through Los Angeles but never got to see any movie stars, Garfield said - and that ought to change. Bette agreed. "The whole idea of the canteen was to give the men fun, relaxation and the chance to meet personally and be served by the stars of Hollywood," she said, "and not to be charged one cent."

To assist them, they recruited Jules Stein, head of the world's largest talent agency, MCA - and other Hollywood stars, guilds, and unions. They found a location for the canteen on Cahuenga Boulevard. The initial capital of $5,000 came from a fund-raising premiere of a Columbia Pictures film. There was also a party at Ciro's restaurant.

The Hollywood Canteen opened October 3, 1942, with 2,000 servicemen entering the door; bleachers were set up outside, and well-heeled spectators paid to watch the stars come and go. Another 5,000 soldiers were turned away because there wasn't enough room. Only servicemen could use the front door. Everyone else - including Hollywood stars - had to use a side entrance.

Bette helped operate the Canteen and took the job seriously – as did the stars who volunteered. They served drinks, washed dishes, and swept the floors. It was an eye-opener to see Marlene Dietrich cooking meals while Kay Francis and Greer Garson waited tables. Director John Ford's wife supervised the kitchen. Dinah Shore, Frank Sinatra, and big-band orchestras performed for free. Bing Crosby brought everyone to tears one Christmas Eve when he showed up to sing with his three young sons.

Bette also found time to continue her movie career, accepting one of her favorite roles that would earn her a record fifth straight Oscar nomination. *Now, Voyager*, based on a novel by Olive Higgins Prouty, tells the story of a mentally and emotionally frail woman who discovers inner strength and independence.

Warner Brothers' Hal Wallis wanted Ginger Rogers to play the female lead but Edmund Goulding, whom the studio had hired to adapt the novel, wanted Irene Dunne. In a display of Bette's clout, however, she convinced Wallis and Jack Warner to bypass all those stars and give her the role. (In another sign of her elevated status, the studio had paid Bette $271,000 the previous year - $4.6 million today - which was even more than it paid Wallis, the company's head of production).

Bette's love interest was played by Paul Henreid, soon to gain lasting fame for his role in *Casablanca,* which debuted in October 1942, just a month after *Now, Voyager.*

Bette and Paul bonded quickly. In his screen test, Henreid was made over so badly by the makeup and costume department - hair slicked flatly to his head, too much stage makeup, and a satin smoking jacket - that he was mortified by the result. So was Bette, who went berserk, screaming that she refused to share the screen with a man who looked like a floorwalker in a department store.

When Bette realized Henreid hated the way he looked, too, they formed a long-lasting friendship, a rarity for Bette when it came to actors of the other sex. Though Hardly a scene went by in which Bette didn't find a reason to argue, Henreid said he enjoyed working with her, later describing her as sociable and complimentary but also genuine.

*Now, Voyager* gave Bette the chance to show off her range. At the beginning of the film, the mental feebleness of her character, Charlotte Vale is revealed as, with nervous hands, she timidly makes her way down the stairs. She is wearing frumpy shoes, a flowered-print dress, no visible makeup, and wire-rimmed glasses, with her drab hair pulled back in a plain style. But after psychotherapy and getting away from her mother's negative influence, Charlotte is transformed. Now she is dressed impeccably in sleek heels with a modern suit and wide-brimmed hat, on a ship heading to South America. But Bette's subtle acting makes it clear the character is still uncertain of herself.

Henreid's performance, meanwhile, had its own impact – in this case, on popular culture. It wasn't what he said in the movie but the way he handled cigarettes: lighting two in his mouth, then handing one to Bette's character. That started a trend of American men imitating the gesture - and often, upon meeting Henreid, asking for a demonstration.

The film - and Henreid's cigarette gymnastics - was a hit for the ages. *Now, Voyager* brought in $2.2 million at the box office ($34 million today) on a budget of

$761,000 - and earned an Oscar nomination for Bette. Though it received mixed reviews at the time, *Now, Voyager* was later ranked twenty-third on the American Film Institutes "100 Years . . . 100 Passions," a list of the top love stories in American cinema.

After *Now, Voyager*, Bette was back to her wartime concerns – this time making a pair of films released in 1943 that addressed the global conflicts head-on. The first, *Watch on the Rhine*, was based on a play by Lillian Hellman, with a screenplay by Hellman's lover, Dashiell Hammett. The film tells of a German named Kurt Muller (Paul Lukas), who vehemently opposes the Nazis and takes his family on a trip to America, where they stay with the parents of his American wife, Sara (Bette). When another house guest, the Romanian count, Teck de Brancovis, threatens to expose Muller's anti-Nazi activities to the Third Reich, Muller kills him.

Wallis sent the screenplay to Davis, a staunch supporter of Franklin D. Roosevelt and a fierce critic of the Nazi Party, and she immediately accepted. But shooting did not go smoothly when it began in mid-June of 1942. *Now, Voyager* had wrapped only a week earlier, and Bette was exhausted and more on edge than usual. She argued with director Herman Shumlin, who had no experience in film. And when Wallis sent Shumlin memos demanding that he tone down Bette's over-emotional performance, she did not appreciate the interference. Bette also clashed with Lucile Watson – who was reprising her stage role as Sara's mother – because she was a Republican with political views Bette vehemently disagreed with.

In the end, however, the film was a success. Bosley Crowther of *The New York Times* called it "a distinguished film - a film full of sense, power and beauty" and *Variety* raved that it was "even better than its powerful original stage version."

Bette's next wartime flick was *Thank Your Lucky Stars*, a fund-raiser for the Hollywood Canteen with an extremely thin plot about a couple of producers trying to put together a charity show while a self-absorbed radio performer (Eddie Cantor) keeps getting in their way.

Bette, playing herself, sang a comical number called "They're Either Too Young or Too Old," about how hard it is to find a man during wartime. (The tune earned an Oscar nomination for composers Frank Loesser and Arthur Schwartz - and later became a hit for Kitty Kallen and the Jimmy Dorsey Orchestra.)

On television years later, Bette described her singing voice as having "more personality than vocal ability, shall we say," which seemed about right to most listeners, and it was the only onscreen musical number of her career. All the actors in *Thank Your Lucky Stars* donated their earnings ($50,000 each) to the Hollywood Canteen.

Following *Thank Your Lucky Stars*, Bette was cast in *Old Acquaintance*, a film that would, once more, contain more drama off-screen than on it thanks to the reappearance of an old adversary. After battling with Miriam Hopkins three years earlier in *The Old Maid*, Bette found herself co-starring with her nemesis once again in this story of two old friends who, ironically enough, feud over a man.

Like the previous film, Bette played against type as the heroine, and Hopkins was the shrew. Later, Bette would theorize that much of Hopkins's unhappiness during both movies stemmed from wanting to be loved as the heroine rather than hated as the nasty character. Tension between them was so high that Bette seemed to look forward to the scene where she had to listen to a speech by Hopkins and then slap her. When it came time to film it, the crew gathered excitedly to witness the spectacle - but Hopkins kept wandering away.

Finally, Bette said, "Miriam! If I have to sit on top of the piano to look into your face for this speech, I will." Hopkins eventually complied, held her ground, and took the hard slap. "To be sure, her eyes filled with tears of self-pity," Bette recalled. Hopkins showed up late the next day, saying she was not feeling well, but somehow, she and Bette managed to complete the film without killing each other.

If a busy movie schedule and volunteer efforts weren't enough, Bette's tumultuous personal life reared its ugly head once again. The culprit this time: the lack of passion Bette felt for her husband, Farney. So, as always, Bette looked elsewhere.

During the filming of *Old Acquaintance* – some two years after her wedding to Farney – she had an affair with her leading man, Gig Young. Young explained his late nights at the studio by telling his wife that Bette and Hopkins were causing delays because they didn't get along. What she didn't know was that he spent some of his off hours in Bette's dressing room - and even at her home, Riverbottom. (Farney was often out of state working with Honeywell and staying involved in the business end of the war effort.)

Bette's affair with Young was short-lived, ending when production for *Old Acquaintance* wrapped up. Young headed off to serve in the Coast Guard, but the two stayed friends.

Young wasn't the only man who snagged Bette's attention during the filming of *Old Acquaintance.* By the end of production, she had a thing for director Vincent Sherman. One Saturday night in February, Jack Warner asked Sherman, Bette, and other members of the crew to stay late to get the movie finished. After working at the studio until 2:00 a.m., Bette asked Sherman for a lift to her mother's house in Laurel Canyon. They stopped at a hamburger joint on the way, and Bette told Sherman that she enjoyed working with him and how much she admired how he handled her conflicts with Hopkins. Then she took his hand and told him that she loved him. But Sherman, who was married, did not pursue her – at least not for the time being.

Clearly, Bette's young marriage to Farney was in trouble. There was no question the couple was fighting a lot around this time. More difficult to determine was whether those fights led to his death – and the controversy that subsequently engulfed Bette's life.

It all started after filming for *Old Acquaintance* concluded in February of 1943, when Bette asked Sherman to come to Mexico with her for an extended vacation. He was sorely tempted but declined, knowing any affair with the volatile Bette would be messy. Farney, learning about Bette's infatuation with the director, confronted him at his office the day before Bette was to leave. Farney told Sherman not to go with her, saying it would be a disaster for all concerned. In fact, he said, he and Bette had had a drunken fight about it the night before.

Bette went to Mexico without either man, instead taking her friend, the Countess Dorothy di Frasso, a prominent Hollywood socialite. Bette called Sherman twice from Mexico, urging him to join her. Again, he declined, saying he was busy with work.

What unfolded shortly thereafter changed Bette's life forever.

On August 23, 1943, Farney left home and went to Walt Disney Studios in Burbank, where he was doing some aeronautical consulting work. Then he did some shopping and met with Bette and his lawyer, Dudley Furse. Afterward, he was walking down busy Hollywood Boulevard, on his way to his car, when he suddenly cried out – "a terrible yell," one witness said – and fell to the pavement. The owner of a tobacco store called an ambulance. Farney was taken to a hospital but never regained consciousness. He died two days later, at age thirty-seven.

When an otherwise healthy man dies suddenly, it can seem bizarre, inexplicable. When that man is the husband of the biggest movie star in the world, it's a big story. Thus began a whirlwind of rumors, suspicion, and investigations by those who believed Bette may have had something to do with his death. The fact that Bette seemed to relish playing devious movie characters who enjoyed murdering their husbands only made Farney's death appear all the more suspicious.

Why? How? The day had begun somewhat typically, Bette recalled, though Farney had been acting odd. In her memoir, *The Lonely Life*, she wrote that "he had been forgetful, disorganized, as he went off to work. He had seemed almost tipsy, and I joked about the possibility that he'd spiked his orange juice. We'd laughed about it. Later on, he'd ordered me a leopard stole at Magnin's. I heard later that while there he was dripping with perspiration."

That day, Bette had been shopping with her hairdresser, Margaret Donovan. She was back home when she got the call about Farney's collapse and immediately called her doctor, Paul Moore, who arranged to meet her at Hollywood Presbyterian hospital. But there was nothing the doctors could do. "It was unbelievable that he was gone - just like that," Bette wrote in her memoir. "And so young. It didn't seem fair. It was my first actual experience with death. I was in a state of real shock."

The autopsy by Dr. Homer Keyes showed that Farney had suffered a basal skull fracture on the right side of his head. Later, during an inquest before a six-man grand jury, Keyes testified that the sidewalk fall was not the cause of death. Arthur Farnsworth, he said, probably died from a blow sustained earlier from "a blunt instrument such as a blackjack or the butt end of a gun" delivered by "some unknown party."

"After receiving some blow to his head," Keyes continued, "Farnsworth had been walking around ever since with the condition fructifying until it eventually caused his death."

On the witness stand, Bette offered an explanation

of what may have happened. In June, while they were at their summer home in New Hampshire, her husband was upstairs and went to answer the telephone, which was downstairs. As he started down the stairs in his stocking feet, he stumbled, landed on his back, and fell the full length of stairs, striking his head. "Although he complained of severe headaches for a day or two," she said, "he seemed to recover quickly and never consulted a doctor."

The problem with this explanation, Dr. Keyes testified, was that his autopsy showed that the original blow to Farney's head had not happened so long ago. It took place, he estimated, "no more than two weeks" before he died.

The grand jury – later reported to be made mostly of men who were big fans of the star – accepted Bette's version of events and did not indict her. Later, in a curious turnabout, Dr. Keyes said, "Following conferences, investigations, hearings, and further medical reports, Bette's explanation was finally accepted as the true one."

So what really happened? Over the years, at least three other possible explanations have surfaced.

In *Bette Davis: More Than a Woman*, author James Spada wrote that according to Bette's third husband, William Grant Sherry, Bette was actually there on Hollywood Boulevard when Farney collapsed. Bette told Sherry that she had been angry at Farney for being drunk and pushed him, causing him to fall and hit his head on the curb. "She could have pushed him and stalked away so quickly that she never realized he had hit his head," Spada surmised.

Others have challenged this theory on several grounds: What about his loud yell before hitting the pavement? Surely, she would have heard it. And how could such a famous star slip away without being noticed on a busy street? Finally, if witnesses did notice her, how could Warner Brothers have convinced them to lie about it under oath, as Spada suggested in his book?

A second theory was advanced by Lawrence Quirk in his book *Fasten Your Seatbelts: The Passionate Life of Bette Davis.* Farney's briefcase, which supposedly disappeared when he collapsed on August 23, reappeared later, filled with liquor bottles – clues to a drunken affair. According to Quirk, Bette "learned that he had been hit over the head two weeks before he died by a husband who had found Farney in bed with his wife."

A third explanation came from Sherman, who said that after Farney died, Bette and Sherman began their affair during the filming of her next movie, *Mr. Skeffington*, which he was directing. Bette invited Sherman into her dressing room for a drink and told him a story, which was recounted in *Dark Victory: The Life of Bette Davis* by Ed Sikov.

The morning she left for Mexico, she and Farney had some drinks and another argument before she left for the train station. He followed her there and climbed onto the train and kept arguing with her after the train had started to move.

"I begged him to get off," Bette told Sherman, "I screamed at him to get off before it was too late, and I pushed him toward the platform. Finally, he took the last few steps down and jumped, but by this time, the train was moving rapidly. I ran down to the bottom step, held onto the bar at the side to look back and see if he was all right. He had fallen and was holding his head."

If that's what really happened, Bette may not have admitted it under oath to avoid charges of involuntary manslaughter for pushing him; to preserve her reputation; or simply to hide her feelings of guilt.

Such unresolved questions kept Farney's death the stuff of tabloids for years. In *The Last Mogul*, a biography of MCA's Lew Wasserman, author Dennis McDougal wrote, "For years afterward, speculation ran rampant through the film colony that Davis had gotten away with murder."

Whatever the truth, Bette seemed to miss her second husband, whose death made her realize that long-term domestic happiness might always elude her. *In The Lonely Life*, she wrote, "He filled the house with his sweetness and consideration of me. Now I was alone again."

But whether Bette learned anything from her nearly four years with Farney – rushing into a marriage to a man she didn't love – remained to be seen. Two years after Farney died, she would marry for the third time.

Once again, it would not be pretty.

# 11
# "I WAS NO LONGER ALONE."

When Farney died, Bette seemed lost.

She embarked on a series of brief affairs and meaningless sexual encounters that did nothing to calm her troubled soul. Even moviemaking provided no sanctuary, as her already outrageous behavior on the set worsened, inspiring acts of revenge by cast and crew alike. When Bette met her next husband, William Sherry, she thought she had finally found the cure for what ailed her. But soon after the wedding, she realized she had made yet another tragic mistake.

This extraordinarily difficult period for Bette began as she mourned the loss of Farney. He had always told Bette that if anything happened to him, he wanted to be buried on Butternut, their gorgeous New Hampshire property. So Bette, Ruthie, Bobby, and Farney's mother took his body back to the land where he had found so much happiness.

Bette decided to create a family cemetery and started blasting rocks and uprooting trees. But Farney's mother, on her visits to the grave, was not satisfied. "We have to remove some trees, Bette," she cried. "My boy can't see the mountains he loved so much!"

When Bette returned to California, Ruthie, now fifty-seven, stayed for the difficult work of moving the family cemetery to Rutland, Vermont. "She knew I couldn't have stood it," she said.

Reeling from Farney's death, Bette plunged into a series of short-term affairs. Some of those quickie romances began at the Hollywood Canteen, according to Lawrence Quirk's biography – a clear violation of Canteen rules that prohibited stars from fraternizing with soldiers. (Director Delmer Daves noted that many of the soldiers were good-looking guys, and said he wouldn't have been surprised if Bette slept with many of them.)

Even with all the beautiful celebrities and other volunteers at the Canteen, Bette often received most of the attention, with servicemen often crowding around her. When the actor Jack Carson asked a Marine why that was, the man used colorful language to indicate that he'd heard Bette was great in the sack.

Bette also met composer Johnny Mercer at the Canteen, which resulted in another brief affair, though it was not publicized at the time. Somehow, she also found time to wash dishes, manage the staff, and perform in stage presentations.

After Farney's death, Bette knew she would need to get back to work eventually. But, not feeling ready yet, she tried to withdraw from her next film, *Mr. Skeffington.* After delaying production to give her time to mourn, Jack Warner finally convinced her to continue, arguing that it would help her recover. The film's director, William Sherman, later claimed that he tried to do his part by sleeping with Bette mainly to get the film completed (their affair ended as soon as production of *Mr. Skeffington* did).

During this difficult time, at least Bette did not have to worry about money. Warner Brothers had given her a new contract that summer, responding to her demands for a higher salary and a limit to the number of films she made each year. Under the new terms, she would have to make just nine films over the next five years. For the first five, she would be paid $115,000 per film ($1.6 million today), and for the last four, she would get $150,000 apiece. A separate agreement stipulated that a new production company Bette had formed, called B.D. Inc., would produce five of her Warner

Brothers movies. That gave her some control over the scripts, though the studio had the final say.

Armed with a new contract, Bette went back to work – "to try and forget" about her grief, she said later. But after the trauma of the previous few months, Bette seemed unhinged. Difficult and demanding even in the best of times, her behavior on the set was now far more erratic and destructive than usual. "In these years I made many enemies," she admitted later. "I was a legendary terror."

*Mr. Skeffington*, based on the novel by Australian writer Elizabeth von Arnim, centers on the life of Fanny, a lovely but egocentric woman (Bette) who marries a well-to-do Jewish man, Job Skeffington, for his money and then proceeds to make him miserable.

Making people miserable came naturally to Bette, who began wreaking havoc early in preproduction. First, she didn't like the version of the script written by John Huston, who had already written and directed *The Maltese Falcon* and was well on his way to becoming a Hollywood legend. That led to the hiring of the screenwriting brothers Julius and Philip Epstein, but they became upset when she began improvising dialogue and demanding immediate rewrites of her scenes.

In the beginning, the studio wanted to film in Technicolor, but settled on black and white after

Bette threw a fit over the color palette. Many more tantrums followed. Sherman said later that her cantankerous behavior on *Old Acquaintance* earlier that year was nothing compared to what he was seeing now. With Bette bossing people around even in scenes she wasn't in, production stalled. Everybody on the set seemed to loathe her. "When people disliked me they really detested me," Bette recalled. "And they couldn't do any more about me than they could about death and taxes."

Things got so bad that Bette was apparently the victim of a cruel prank. When she tried to apply eyewash, she cried out in pain. The container had been filled with a highly flammable, corrosive liquid called aceteyne, used by welders. "It almost dissolved my eyes," Bette said later. "I screamed in agony." Her makeup artist quickly washed her eyes with castor oil, but Bette did not film that day. She preferred to believe, she said in her memoir, that it was all an innocent mistake. But when detectives investigated, Sherman told them, "If you asked everyone on the set who would have committed such a thing, everyone would raise their hand!"

By early January of 1944, production for Mr. Skeffington was an entire month behind schedule and tension was thick. When the Epstein brothers got a memo from Jack Warner asking why *Mr. Skeffington* was taking so long, they cracked that their director, Bette Davis, was sluggish. At one point, Warner became enraged that Bette refused to re-shoot some scenes and stormed off to confront her. But once he was face-to-face with her, he was all charm, calling her darling and giving her a hug. Clearly, their relationship had come a long way from the days when Warner had the upper hand, forcing her to make terrible movies that she hated.

*Mr. Skeffington* finally wrapped on February 21, and the film was a hit, grossing $208 million in domestic box-office revenue. Bette received yet another Academy Award nomination, her seventh. Perhaps more importantly, Bette and Warner Brothers got a much-needed break from each other. With her new contract reducing her workload, Bette would make only one other film in 1944 – a cameo in a musical comedy trifle called *The Hollywood Canteen* – and by then, fortunately for everyone who had to work with her, she seemed a bit more settled. In fact, her only film in 1945, *The Corn Is Green*, displayed a relatively cooperative Bette on the set, and many of her suggestions improved the film (which earned a profit of $2.2 million ($30 million today).

Bette's improved behavior at this time may have had something to do with her new romantic interests.

While filming *The Corn Is Green*, she went to a party in Laguna Beach, where Ruthie lived, and met a painter and masseur named William Sherry. He brought her a drink and charmed her by claiming he had no idea who she was and therefore would not be intimidated by her.

But as Sherry pursued her – "no one ever paid court with the singularity of purpose that Sherry displayed," she said later – Bette was having an affair with another man, Corporal Lewis A. Riley, an officer with the U.S. Army Signal Corps. She met Riley in Los Angeles, where he worked in military communications making training films. By fall, Riley was stationed at Fort Benning, Georgia, where Bette planned to visit him. Not everyone in Bette's circle was enamored of Riley, however. Jack Warner's wife Ann told Bette not to bother with him. She was a celebrity, Ann told her, and he was merely a man who made khaki look fantastic.

Bette ignored her advice. In September, she went to Georgia to see Cpl. Riley and denied rumors that the couple planned to wed. "I am not going to marry anyone," she told the *Atlanta Constitution*. The locals around Fort Benning were well aware of her visit. In *Photoplay*, Pauline Swanson reported that autograph-seeking fans were camped at the padlocked gate of the vacation home in nearby Phenix City, Alabama, where she was staying. She had brought four dogs with her, and they could be seen walking around outside. One fan attached a note to the collar of her collie and was delighted when the dog returned with an autograph, as requested. The town was abuzz with any detail about Bette's stay, including the fact that she spent $25 on fancy groceries from Mr. Otis Taft's grocery store.

Bobby visited her in Georgia, and tried but failed to keep away the reporters and photographers who swarmed around the house. Finally, Bette emerged and posed for pictures wearing a red and white plaid shirt and navy blue knee-length shorts. "Bette took to life in Phenix City like a native," Swanson noted in her article. "She carried wood from the back yard for the fireplace and the wood-burning cook stove . . . She bought hip boots and overalls and joined her farmer neighbors in fishing expeditions and coon and possum hunts."

Around this time, Bette's relationship with Riley inadvertently got her invited to a special dinner with none other than her idol, President Franklin Roosevelt. Having campaigned that fall to help him win a fourth term, she wanted to meet him - and wrangled an invitation to the White House. But Bette was just one guest of many. As she stood in a line of admirers on October 19, 1944, Roosevelt made his way toward her and extended his hand. Then he recognized her and said, laughing, "And how did you get into this mob, Miss Davis?"

"I wrote, Mr. President, asking to meet you and I received this invitation," she said.

"This is ridiculous," he said. "What are you doing

at a public tea? How long are you going to be in Washington?"

"I'm just here to see you. I'm vacationing with friends in Georgia."

The mention of Georgia gave him an idea. "I'm leaving for Warm Springs for my first visit in a long time. Will you give me another chance to play host?"

It was an incredible coincidence, and Bette was thrilled to soon receive an official invitation to a Thanksgiving dinner at the president's estate in Warm Springs, Georgia, thirty-five miles north of Riley's outpost at Fort Benning. When she arrived, she could see that a number of guests - like the president himself - were wheelchair-bound, either as a result of war injuries or polio or infantile paralysis. Still, she did not hesitate in maneuvering her way to a seat next to the president, accompanied by her boyfriend, Cpl. Riley.

As the party wore on, Bette monopolized Roosevelt's time, to the annoyance of White House staffers and the head of the Georgia Warm Springs Foundation. William D. Hassett, Roosevelt's personal aide, mentioned it in his diary entry for November 28, 1944, saying that everyone was shocked that the actress had flattered her way past the foundation administrator to sit next to the president. The movie star didn't seem to care about the disapproving glances. It was, she said later, a glorious "night to remember," especially in retrospect, since Roosevelt passed away the following April.

After the high of their presidential visit, Bette's relationship with Riley came down to earth. She did not mention him by name in either of her memoirs, but was clearly referring to Riley in her second book, *This 'N That*, when she discussed problems she was having with "a man I thought I might marry." With World War II still raging, Riley was sent to Europe, then transferred to Japan. Before he left, he asked Bette to wait for him. "If that's what you really want," she told him, "you should put a diamond on my finger."

He did not. Once he was gone, Bette became more involved with Sherry, who had been recently discharged by the Marines. But this deepening relationship led to family warfare, as both Ruthie and Bobby mistrusted Sherry and were adamantly against her seeing him. Perversely, that pushed them even closer as Bette became determined to prove them wrong.

Later, Bette realized that he had made up his mind to marry her the moment they met – possibly even before that - which was fine with her since she was used to being adored by fans from afar. "This is it," she told herself. "He is dedicated. He's a worker. He'll become a fine painter and he worships me. It doesn't matter that he has no money. Sherry is an artist. These middle-class concepts mean as little to him as to me. What drive the man has!"

But Ruthie's drive to separate them was nearly as strong. By now ensconced in upscale Hollywood life, Ruthie was aghast that Sherry's mother was an elevator operator in a hotel in San Diego – and told Bette that a woman of her station should not be consorting with such low-brow types.

Bobby, meanwhile, hired a private detective to investigate Sherry – but Bette refused to read his damning report. Later, she guessed at what the sleuth might have discovered, things she herself would find out too late: Sherry's hair-trigger temper, his struggles to support himself, and his longstanding scheme to marry someone rich. A friend informed her later that Sherry had told his Marine buddies in San Diego that when he left the service, his goal was to marry a wealthy woman.

While this family drama was going on, sixty-year-old Ruthie was also getting involved with a questionable character, a fifty-three-year-old businessman from Belmont, Massachusetts, named Robert Woodbury Palmer. They met at Smoke Tree Ranch in Palm Springs and soon afterward, in November of 1945, were married, with Bette as maid of honor. But something did not seem quite right about him. According to a newspaper clipping found in Bette's archives, Palmer had gone to Reno ten days prior to divorce his previous wife, Helen Bush Palmer - and had met Ruthie only a few weeks before marrying her. He and his ex had been married thirty-two years and had two children, the article said, adding a revealing coda: Many of their friends in Belmont had no idea they were even divorced.

The marriage did not last long. Whether Palmer, like Sherry, was involved in an elaborate scheme – possibly in cahoots with his ex-wife – to marry into the Davis family money remains an open question. But clearly, both mother and daughter were not very good judges of character.

Meanwhile, Bette was busy making her own mistakes.

Despite her family's protestations, she decided to marry Sherry, whose artistic drive led her to believe they had much in common. Perhaps more to the point, she added that there was not a surplus of men around during the war years. "I justified this dreadful mistake in many ways," she said later of her decision to remarry at the age of thirty-seven. "I was lonely and restless and had been a widow for two years."

Bette and Sherry were married on November 29, 1945, in the chapel of Mission Inn, a hotel in Riverside, California. Ruthie's new husband, Robert Palmer, gave the bride away. With her family so staunchly opposed to the marriage, it was hardly surprising that *The New York Times* reported Bette seemed uncomfortable during the ceremony and "somewhat flustered" while walking down the aisle. But gossip columnist Hedda Hopper swooned over Sherry, writing that he had a magnetic smile and looked like a "handsome Greek god."

"This time, all would be well," Bette told herself. "Sherry had his work, I had mine. His adoration of me, quite naturally, excited me. I was no longer alone."

After she said her vows, Bette threw her bouquet to Bobby, who caught it. The ancient ritual seemed to do the trick. Soon, Bobby married a man named David Berry whom she had met in Laguna. For a brief period, all three of the Davis women were married and, by all outward appearances, all was well.

Except that, of course, it wasn't.

It turns out that Sherry, a former prizefighter, enjoyed hitting people outside the ring as well – and Bette became a regular target. The abuse started when they drove to Mexico for their honeymoon. "En route my husband threw me out of the car for some forgotten reason," she said later. "This was only the beginning."

After each outburst, Sherry apologized, but then returned to his violent ways. Not nearly as successful in his creative pursuits as she was, he would lash out in frustration. Bette was far more consumed with her film work than she was with

Sherry, which also upset him. He wanted to be the center of her life but never was.

For a while, Bette blamed herself for not being more emotionally available to her husband. But soon enough, she realized the problem went far deeper. She had married a dangerous man whom she hardly knew – and what she did know about him was troubling. "I was possessed with my career," she said later. "Sherry was possessed with me."

# 12

# "THE PERFECT SETTING, I DECIDED, IN WHICH TO KILL MYSELF."

Life rarely remained settled for Bette Davis. In the frenetic five-year period of the late 1940s, she managed to have a baby, nearly commit suicide, get divorced, and release a couple of hit movies along with three outright stinkers that sent her career into a wild tailspin after so many years of celebrated success.

It was a period that started out full of promise in 1945, as the war ended and Bette embarked on what she hoped would be a fulfilling and lucrative new role: movie producer. She lined up a drama called *A Stolen Life,* which would be the first film produced by her new company, B.D. Productions. It would also be the last.

Bette played two parts in the movie – the twin sisters Kate and Patricia, who were in love with the same man. As shooting got underway, Bette bossed people around, as always, and clashed with nearly everyone, especially director Curtis Bernhardt. In that sense, being a producer was no different than being a temperamental star. "If that was producing," she once said, "I had been a mogul for years."

And, just as with many of her movies, there were delays. Production was set back when Bette and other cast and crew continually called in sick; it did not wrap until late July, thirty-three days behind schedule. *A Stolen Life* received poor reviews when it was released the following summer, in July of 1946. Bosley Crowther of *The New York Times* called it "a distressingly empty piece." But, still, it was one of Bette's biggest box-office successes, raking in profits of $2.5 million. In fact, the U.S. Treasury would name Davis as the highest paid woman in the country in 1947, with her producer's share of profit from *A Stolen Life* accounting for most of those earnings.

Despite that financial bonanza, it was clear that being a producer was not Bette's forte. She and Warner Brothers agreed in February of 1946 to a new contract that eliminated the producing clauses, and B.D. Productions was liquidated the following year.

Bette's new contract covered nearly three-and-a-half

years - 172 weeks, expiring in 1949 - and allowed her to slow down her pace, requiring no more than eight pictures during that period. She would be paid well at $6,000 per week (nearly $80,000 now) for the first sixty-six weeks, and $7,000 weekly after that. She also received permission to make unlimited radio appearances as long as the programs were not adaptations of films made at competing studios.

But no sooner had the ink dried on Bette's new contract than her steep career descent began, thanks to her next movie, *Deception*. It was the story of a pianist (Bette) who thinks her cellist fiancé has been killed in battle and takes up with a wealthy composer. It looked like a sure winner, largely because of the co-stars: Paul Henreid, the fiancé, and Claude Rains, the composer. By now, both were quite famous as the *Casablanca* duo who had teamed up so successfully with Bette in *Now, Voyager*.

But, once again, Bette's mercurial behavior put the film far behind schedule. There was a minor car accident; a cold; strep throat; a finger injury; a substitute cameraman whom Bette refused to work with. In addition, a fight about her working hours resulted in her calling in sick the next day, triggering a brief suspension (that single lost day of shooting cost the studio nearly $6,500, or $86,000 today. In total, Bette missed seventeen days, and *Deception* ran forty-six days late.

Though the film received generally positive reviews, high production costs caused by the delays, combined with surprisingly weak ticket sales, made it the first Bette Davis movie – ever - to lose money.

How many of Bette's missed days on *Deception* were caused by fights with her husband was unclear, but their young marriage was clearly foundering. Sherry forbade Bette's mother from showing up unannounced, as was her habit, and told his wife to stop letting Ruthie run her life. As Bette stopped confiding in her mom, she said later, Ruthie's "distrust and disapproval of Sherry now became loathing."

Tensions worsened, largely because Bette was raking in big bucks while sales of Sherry's paintings foundered. And he continued to abuse her – often, she said, for no apparent reason. "Out of the blue, he could become a monster," Bette recalled. Then, minutes after a tirade, he would behave as if nothing had happened.

Bette often considered leaving him during that first year together. But, she said later, "One does not give up easily on a third marriage. I was not eager to admit that I had failed once again in my choice of a husband, with all the inevitable publicity."

Then, suddenly, all thoughts of divorce evaporated: Bette had become pregnant. It happened in the latter stages of the tortured filming of *Deception* and rumors immediately started swirling that Paul Henreid was the father. It irked Henreid terribly that Bette encouraged them. He wasn't sure why she did that but guessed it was to get revenge on her abusive husband. Whatever the reason, she would tell friends of Henreid's that she had a crush on him and wanted to start an affair. At first, the whole thing seemed like a joke, but it sparked rumors that persisted to the point that Henreid and his wife were thoroughly annoyed.

For Bette, it seemed like a twisted game. When Henreid and Bette were in her dressing room rehearsing their lines, she would see her husband coming and quickly lock the door and yell that she and Henreid were busy inside and wanted to be left alone. Henreid didn't think it was funny, especially considering the temper and strength of her husband, the ex-boxer. One day, Sherry got so mad he started shaking the trailer.

Though Bette's marriage to Sherry was tempestuous, to say the least, she wanted to have the child this time. In October, she informed Warner Brothers that come December, she would need to take an unspecified amount of time off for personal reasons. It was by now obvious what that reason was, and the studio agreed to keep her on salary during her absence.

With their family growing, Bette and Sherry

decided to buy a house at Wood's Cove in Laguna Beach, which she filled with antiques and her precious books. Perched on a bluff overlooking the Pacific, the place had a large living room where Sherry set up an area to paint and hang his artwork, mostly landscapes and still-life pieces.

Getting the house in order made the days pass quickly.

*Time* covered the baby's birth on May 1, 1947: "Born. To Bette Davis, thirty-nine, high-strung cinema actress, and painter (ex-boxer) William Grant Sherry, thirty-two, her third husband: her first child, a girl, on May Day, which Bette Davis chose for her Cesarean section; in Santa Ana, Calif. Name: Barbara Davis Sherry. Weight: 7 lbs."

Sherry had wanted a son, but Bette was thrilled it was a girl. The baby was named after Bette's sister, whose birth name was Barbara. Bette and Sherry called her B.D., which they pronounced "beady."

"And for the first time in my life," Bette said later, "I became a willing slave to another human being." As she lavished attention on her baby, she could feel that this tiny, helpless, gorgeous creature had transformed her in ways she could barely understand. She still had her career, but suddenly work didn't seem quite as important anymore. "My life seemed full without it."

Even her husband seemed to have changed.

"Fatherhood was good for Sherry," she recalled. "He worshiped B.D. and all was well for a while."

Not a single Bette Davis movie was released that year, as she adjusted to motherhood – the first year that had happened since she started her Hollywood career sixteen years earlier. But she came back with two movies in 1948 – *Winter Meeting* and *June Bride*. The former was a tedious drama of passing love, based on a novel by Grace Zaring Stone, that received terrible reviews after the original story was decimated to gain the approval of Hollywood censors. It was Bette's second film in a row to lose money, and Jack Warner began to wonder if his normally profitable star had lost her touch.

*June Bride*, by contrast, was a comedy with Bette well-cast as a magazine editor from New York who is reunited with an old flame played by Robert Montgomery. It was well received – *Time* called it "the best Bette Davis picture in some time" – and made enough money to put Bette back in Warner's good graces. He would give her a new, four-picture contract with an increased salary of $10,285 a week ($116,000 now).

But, as if the stress of balancing motherhood with film acting wasn't enough, Bette also had to deal with the return of Sherry's abuse. Fatherhood, it turned out, hadn't changed him at all. One day, he threw her down some steps onto their front lawn. That was it. With the help of her makeup man and good friend Perc Westmore, Bette finally escaped her violent husband, moving with B.D. into a two-story apartment.

The move did little, however, to improve Bette's bad mood. In fact, her new home was "[the] perfect setting, I decided, in which to kill myself."

In her memoir, *This 'N That*, Bette insisted that she was quite serious. "I didn't want to live this way any longer," she wrote. "How could I deal with such a man? I was even afraid to divorce him. I was not accustomed to being afraid of someone I lived with. I was desperate."

Bette planned every detail of her suicide, even picking out the nightgown she would wear. She would overdose on sleeping pills. She imagined the scene the next morning: When she did not appear on set at 9:00 a.m. as scheduled, the cast and crew would break into her dressing room and find her lying there. Tearful, whispered words would ricochet around the set: *Bette Davis is dead!*

Bette solemnly took out all the pills she had – the ones she used occasionally when she had trouble sleeping – and lined them all up. Then she started laughing. And laughed some more. "This is ridiculous," she told herself. "This is just not your bag at all." She thought about her daughter. "Could I do that to her?" She put away the pills.

When Sherry promised to see an analyst, Bette

gave him another chance. But nothing changed. One evening, for no apparent reason, he threw a silver ice bucket at her, Bette said. She was holding B.D., then just six months old. (Sherry denied it.) "I had told Sherry if he ever showed any violence toward B.D. I would leave him," she said later. "I did, once and for all."

Sherry, of course, had his own version of what was happening between them. Bette found the violence exciting, he said, and was not exactly innocent herself. In what sounded like a bizarre dominance-and-submission game, she mocked his aspirations and belittled him - mostly because she liked working him up into a furious state, he said. That way, he would have a chance to prove that he could control her.

He recalled a particularly bitter argument about money when she went on and on about how worthless he was in contributing to the family income. She called him a kept boy, getting him so worked up that he turned the dining room table - dishes and all - over on her. Then he left her trapped under the table. Somehow, she got out, and they had makeup sex that night. In their sadomasochistic exercise, neither one succeeded in dominating the other.

By 1949, both her marriage and her relationship with Warner Brothers were clearly crumbling. Her new contract with the studio did not give Bette the power to choose her roles, and she hated the new script she was assigned, a film called *Beyond the Forest*. Though she liked the novel by Stuart Engstrand that it was based upon, she had enough experience with Hollywood censors to know that any film version would have to be watered down beyond recognition.

Indeed, Joseph Breen of the Production Code Administration refused to approve the script, and it was easy to see why: Its protagonist, Rosa Moline (Bette), was a malicious woman who schemed against her own marriage, was savage in her lust, and was capable of attempted abortion and murder. Not even the end of the story promoted morality, Breen complained.

In what turned out to be her last visit to his office, Bette begged Warner not to make her play Rosa. As always, she wore sunglasses so he could not look into her eyes. Unmoved, Warner insisted she play the part.

In retrospect, the studio chief should have listened to his star. When *Beyond the Forest* came out in October of 1949, the reviews were scathing. For example: Dorothy Manners of the *Los Angeles Examiner* called the film "an unfortunate finale to her brilliant career." Gossip columnist Hedda Hopper wrote, "If Bette had deliberately set out to wreck her career, she could not have picked a more appropriate vehicle."

The film's only saving grace was the iconic moment when Bette as Rosa walks downstairs, surveys her living room, and says, "What a dump." Playwright Edward Albee would incorporate that into his classic *Who's Afraid of Virginia Woolf?* later made into a film starring Elizabeth Taylor. Taylor played Martha, who spends a great deal of time trying to recall the movie in which Bette Davis says that line. (Many years later, Bette Davis impersonators used it in their acts and Bette herself would get plenty of laughs by making it her opening line at speaking engagements.)

For Bette, the straw that broke the camel's back in her relationship with Warner Brothers came while filming a scene in *Beyond the Forest,* which required her to throw a medicine bottle. In the ensuing fight with Director King Vidor over exactly how she should toss the prop, Bette insisted that Vidor be fired over the matter – and if he wasn't, she demanded to be released from her contract. Refusing to let Vidor go, Warner decided he had had enough of Bette's histrionics that inevitably led to costly delays – especially since her films were bombing. So he finally called her bluff and agreed to nullify the contract.

For her part, Bette had had enough of making lousy movies. After making fifty-two films in eighteen years for Warner Brothers – and becoming one of the biggest stars in Hollywood – she felt she had earned the right to choose her own roles. "I felt that if after all my fighting for the right scripts they were still giving me the wrong ones, there was no longer any point," she said later.

Fittingly, her last words spoken on the Warner Brothers lot, while recording the soundtrack for *Beyond the Forest*, were these: "I can't stand it here anymore."

And yet the studio had been her home for nearly her entire career. Now a forty-one-year-old actress with an uncertain future, she cried when she drove home that night. "Those years," said later, "were the greatest of my life."

As gossip columnists concluded that Bette Davis's career was over, she found herself glad to be able to spend time at the beach with her daughter – and bring her to see Grandma Ruthie. She also tried again to patch things up with Sherry, but his abuse continued.

Some of her stories about Sherry's behavior seemed ripped from a 1940s film-noir screenplay. In one improbable tale recounted in her memoir, *This 'N That,* Bette claimed that Sherry had been plotting against her with B.D.'s twenty-one-year-old nanny, Marion Richards, with whom he was having an affair. One day, according to Bette, the housekeeper happened to pick up the phone and heard Sherry devising a plan with Richards, who was on the other extension, to have B.D. kidnapped and demand a ransom. He specified the street and time, saying ominously, "Bring B.D."

When the housekeeper told Bette, she was aghast. She raced home and had her bodyguard grill and threaten Richards, but she refused to admit anything. "I no longer had a reason, if any ever existed, to delay leaving Sherry once and for all," Bette wrote. "I had sent him to analysts, had overlooked so much, all for the sake of a marriage that meant nothing to him."

Bette doesn't say how Sherry reacted to the charge that he plotted to kidnap his own daughter – or whether she called the police – but he denied it when the allegation became public. But Sherry clearly did have an affair with Richards, whom he would later marry.

After that alleged incident, Bette hired a prominent Hollywood attorney to renew divorce proceedings. She also tried to go back to work, but her personal problems followed here there, too, when she teamed up with Curtis Bernhardt, her director for *A Stolen Life*, to make her first post-Warner Brothers film. The title? Appropriately, *The Story of a Divorce* (the name was later changed to *Payment on Demand*).

When the film wrapped in April of 1950, the cast and crew gave Bette a surprise party for her forty-second birthday. Having behaved herself on the set this time, she was given a huge ostrich egg. (Yes, for being "a good egg.") But Sherry, still trying to win her back, showed up at the party, uninvited. When Bette asked the security guards to keep him out, Sherry decided to put his boxing skills to use and started a fight. Bette's co-star Barry Sullivan intervened, and Sherry punched him to the ground.

As the press covered the story, Sherry saw a chance to share his woes. The life of a stay-at-home husband had been hard, he said. He had to have dinner ready when she got home, bring her slippers and fix her drinks, only to be refused affection because she was too exhausted.

A few months later, Bette was granted a divorce from Sherry in Juárez, Mexico. Soon afterward, Sherry married the former nanny. As part of the divorce settlement, Sherry received alimony from Bette for three years. "I wanted out," she said later, "and money made it possible."

After such a tumultuous marriage, one might think Bette would take some time to heal and recover – but no.

Twenty-five days after her divorce, she would marry a man she had met only a few months earlier, during the shooting of her next film, the classic *All About Eve*. Gary Merrill, her handsome leading man in that film, would become her fourth husband – and her last chance to find out whether it was possible for her to live happily ever after. It would not be smooth going. As Bette's *All About Eve* character, Margo Channing, famously said, "Fasten your seatbelts, it's going to be a bumpy night."

# 13

# "THERE WAS NO QUESTION THAT WE LOVED AND RESPECTED EACH OTHER. HOW COULD WE FAIL?"

*All About Eve* would become a watershed moment for Bette. Not only did she meet her future husband on the set – her ten years with Gary Merrill would be the longest of her four marriages – but she created, in Margo Channing, one of the screen's greatest characters in an iconic film that re-ignited her career. She also proved she could succeed as a freelancer, beyond the reach of the oppressive studio system.

After being released from her contract by Warner Brothers, Bette was frightened by her newfound freedom – she compared it to leaving home for the first time – but also thrilled that she was finally able to make any movie she wanted. Or at least any project she could put together, which in

Hollywood is never easy, even for established stars. The unpredictability of her new existence became clear when *Payment on Demand*, her first film as a solo artist, was filmed in 1949, but not released until 1951 – a long time for a movie star to wait when she is trying to remain in the public eye.

Fortunately, another golden opportunity came along in the interim. While shooting *Payment on Demand,* Bette got a call from the producer Darryl Zanuck, who offered to send her a script if she would promise to read it right away. The call came as quite a surprise. She had not spoken to Zanuck in the nine years since she abruptly resigned as president of the Academy of Motion Picture Arts and Sciences.

However, time and circumstances had changed everything. Claudette Colbert had been cast as Margo in *All About Eve* but had seriously injured her back. Zanuck needed an A-list replacement – and quickly. The filmmakers had access to the Curran Theater in San Francisco for only two weeks to shoot the interior and exterior scenes in this drama about a fading Broadway star. Filming had to begin in ten days, giving Bette only five days to prepare after *Payment on Demand* was completed. "It all sounded impossible and why worry?" Bette thought. "It probably was a lousy script anyway."

How wrong she was. Bette was immediately dazzled by the screenplay and told Zanuck she would do whatever it took to make this happen. She quickly met with director Joseph Mankiewicz, worked with costume designer Edith Head, and did a full-dress film test at 20th Century Fox.

When word got around that Mankiewicz planned to hire Bette, he was inundated with phone calls from people she had worked with; most of them said, essentially, "Are you nuts?!" The writer and director Edmund Goulding, who had worked with Bette previously, warned that she would reduce him to dust. She would not only bring a yellow pad and pencils to rewrite scenes but would direct them as well. Willie Wyler, on the other hand, told Mankiewicz that he would have a ball working with her.

Wyler, it turns out, was right. *All About Eve* is centered around a conniving young woman named Eve Harrington, played by Anne Baxter. Eve conjures up a false life story, riddled with hardships, to scheme her way into the life of her favorite theater actress, Margo Channing, Bette's character. Before long, Eve is blackmailing her way into a leading role that had originally been written for the aging Margo - until the writer Addison DeWitt (George Sanders) unearths Eve's true history and uses it against her in the end.

For Bette, playing a forty-year-old actress now past her prime hit very close to home. "Margo Channing was a woman I understood thoroughly," Bette said later. Like Bette, Margo had realized that fame and fortune meant nothing without a man to come home to. Playing Margo forced Bette to confront what she called "the unholy mess of my own life - another divorce, my permanent need for love, my aloneness." As she played the scenes, she said, "I had hard work to remember I was playing a part. . . . keeping the tears back was not an easy job."

Professionally and artistically, however, it was a near-perfect experience. "I can think of no project that from the outset was as rewarding from the first day to the last," Bette said later. She cited the clever script and masterful direction by Mankiewicz - and a first-rate cast that, in addition to Merrill, Baxter, and Sanders, also featured Celeste Holm as Margo's close friend Karen Richards.

*All About Eve* has been celebrated, analyzed, and chronicled by film lovers to an exhausting degree over the years. Its worthiness, however, is hard to deny. Today, the movie review website Rotten Tomatoes gives it a perfect 100 percent score. Upon its release in October 1950, Bosley Crowther of *The New York Times* called it "a withering satire - witty, mature and worldly-wise" and "a boundless tribute to Mr. Mankiewicz and his cast for ranging a gallery of people that dazzle, horrify and fascinate."

The film was nominated for fourteen Academy Awards – a feat matched by only two later movies (1997's *Titanic* and 2016's *La La Land*) – and won six trophies, including Best Picture. Bette was nominated for an Oscar but did not prevail that year - Judy Holliday won it for *Born Yesterday* - but she did take home Best Actress from the Cannes Film Festival and the New York Film Critics Circle Award.

When *All About Eve* hit the theaters, Bette told Mankiewicz how grateful she was that he had given her a new life, both professionally and personally. She was also thankful that Claudette Colbert had hurt her back. "On what strange circumstances are whole lives changed," she said later. "No broken back - no Gary Merrill."

Merrill played Margo's love interest, the director Bill Sampson. Bette had never met the actor before but, strangely enough, had an enormous fight with Sherry over him about a year earlier. On New Year's Eve, they had rented a house on Lake Arrowhead in California's San Bernardino mountains and brought along their toddler B.D. and the nanny Sherry would later marry. Bette and Sherry decided to go see a film that night, *Twelve O'clock High,* starring Merrill. When Bette raved about what a wonderful actor he was – and so attractive! – Sherry became jealous. All the way home, they had a huge argument about it.

When Bette finally met Merrill on the set in the spring of 1950, the sparks were immediate. Both were still married at the time, Merrill to an actress named Barbara Leeds. According to Celeste Holm, the cast was out having drinks one night when Bette and Merrill took one look at each other, and that was that.

As they became acquainted, their romance seemed like fate. Merrill had vacationed as a child at Prout's Neck, Maine, near Ocean Park, where Bette had spent summers as a child. He went to the Loomis Chaffee boarding school in Windsor, Connecticut, where Bette knew the headmaster, Frank Grubbs.

When filming wrapped, Bette and Merrill decided to get married right away. But that was no simple matter since they both already *had* spouses. So they headed to Mexico, the preferred destination for quickie divorces. They were married in Juárez on July 28, 1950, the same day Merrill's divorce was finalized.

"I sensed in Gary my last chance at love and marriage," Bette said later. "I wanted these as desperately as ever. I had been an actress first and a woman second. I had proved what I wanted to prove about the actress part."

That second part, about succeeding in her personal life, would remain problematic, however. Things started out well, as they often did for Bette. The blissful couple headed up to New England for their honeymoon - and, at Merrill's suggestion, they were soon joined by B.D. at Robin Hood Island, north of Bath, Maine. Bette was deeply touched that her new husband wanted her three-year-old child there. They had chosen that rugged area because it was near Squirrel Island, where Bette's mother and father had honeymooned – and where Bette, she was told, had been conceived.

Around this time, Bette wasn't the only one in the family racking up marriages. Her mother had sent her a telegram in April saying that she had married a man named Captain O. W. Budd in Immanuel Community Church in Las Vegas. This marriage, her third, lasted less than two years, until the end of 1951.

Ruthie's other daughter also had her marriage woes. Bobby had divorced her second husband, David Berry, in 1949, after marrying him only two years earlier. Fay Pelgram, Bobby's daughter by her first husband, was ten years old when that divorce occurred, and she would later say that though Berry was kind to her, he drank too much. (At one point, Bobby threw him out of the house and obtained a restraining order against him. After their divorce, Bobby experienced another lapse and remained in a mental hospital for the next two years.)

During their honeymoon in Maine, Bette and Merrill got to work on one of the vows they had made before marrying: that they would adopt children together. They called a doctor to register their interest, and then Merrill headed off to shoot a film in the Virgin Islands. Soon afterward, as Bette was staying in Westport, Connecticut, at the home of her friend Robin Brown, she was notified that a baby girl was available – immediately. The next day, Bette and Merrill had their first child together.

Merrill was a little shocked when Bette told him by phone that he had become a father so soon – especially because he thought they had agreed to adopt a boy first. But he came to love the girl, who had been born in January 1951 to an unmarried alcoholic. As they made lists of baby names, Merrill came up with Margo. "Of course," Bette thought. "How perfect!" But they added a "t," so the baby's name became Margot Mosher Merrill.

When Bette brought the baby home, she told B.D. to close her eyes; she had a special present for her. Then she placed the real-live doll in the girl's arms. "Her eyes when she opened them had all the wonders of the universe," Bette recalled later. "She had a sister."

Back in California, Bette began searching for a bigger house for their growing family and found one in Malibu. Merrill, who had finished his Virgin Islands film, *Frogmen*, was already off to Germany to shoot the World War II drama, *Decision Before Dawn*. So Bette moved Merrill's belongings into their new place. Finally, Merrill returned to his new home – and his new wife, two daughters, a housekeeper named Dell, a baby nurse, and a governess for B.D.

"The walls that night rang with love, laughter and a closeness of two people who had each found what they had always looked for," Bette said later. "I had such respect for Gary and was so proud to be his wife. The next few months were the happiest we ever had. Storm signals every now and then of the tragedy to come - but soon forgotten in the overall compatibility. He loved Margot. It was his first own daughter. He took care of her often - diapers and all. God was in his heaven."

Professionally, Bette was entering what she would later call her Black Years. Spanning the entire 1950s and then some – until *What Ever Happened to Baby Jane?* in 1962 – this period was dominated by critical derision and lousy films, many of which lost money. It also coincided with the gradual disintegration of her marriage to Merrill.

One reason her films were not successful is that Bette no longer seemed to view her movie projects as noble artistic pursuits; they were gravy trains. The string of bad films began with *Another Man's Poison*, a British murder mystery wholly lacking in suspense. The lead role had originally been offered to Gloria Swanson, after her huge success with *Sunset Boulevard*, but Swanson wisely turned it down. Bette accepted it in large part for the chance to travel to Great Britain for the shooting. And for the money. She not only earned £40,000 ($1.5 million today) but insisted that her new husband play opposite her.

The Davis-Merrill family boarded the Queen Elizabeth with B.D., now four years old, two-month-old Margot, and their staff of three, and headed for Southampton, England. No sooner had they arrived than Bette revealed herself as the vainglorious, out-of-touch Hollywood star she had become.

Before they got off the boat, Bette invited the British press to their suite for hors d'oeuvres and drinks. That was a mistake. In their columns, they described her as middle-aged and matronly and noted her excess of luggage and fur coats. Moreover, the reporters insisted on calling Merrill "Mr. Davis," which infuriated Bette.

The filming itself, from April to June of 1951, was more like a luxury family vacation than a serious attempt to make a great film. Bette and family stayed at Great Fosters, a hotel in Surrey that had been a hunting lodge used by Henry VIII and Elizabeth I, whom Bette had portrayed twelve years prior.

The reviews, not surprisingly, were scathing: According to the *New Statesman*, Bette was "a blaze of breathtaking absurdity," and the *Socialist Leader* said Merrill "wanders about looking like a cross between Tarzan and Frankenstein." The film failed at the box office, and Hollywood columnists announced that Bette's comeback was fizzling out.

Indeed, Bette seemed more interested in expanding

her family than making films. Only a year after adopting Margot, she and Merrill decided to adopt the boy he always wanted. They brought Michael Woodman Merrill home from the Los Angeles hospital just a few days after he was born on February 5, 1952.

Soon enough, Merrill would also adopt B.D. – though Bette's ex-husband Sherry only agreed to relinquish custody after she withheld his final alimony payment, refusing to pay until he relented. With that maneuver, Bette and Merrill now had three children.

But their marriage, not even two years old, was already fraying. Some of the tensions between them, early in the marriage, seemed minor at the time. Merrill would work like crazy and then just stop and lie around in bed for two straight weeks at a time. Bette could not understand such laziness and was frustrated by his careless attitude toward his career. ("I had no drive, really," Merrill once admitted to an interviewer. "I just like to get by and have fun.")

As they created a family together, the problems became deeper. Merrill was "mean and unpleasant" with B.D., Bette said, which she surmised was because he considered the girl Bette's child rather than his own. He was also absent for long periods while he shot films. "Gary's great desire was to be a free soul - no responsibility," Bette said later.

In another sign of trouble, Bette began to notice that her husband was, in some ways, like her own, distant father – "cynical, bright, negative and earthbound." Merrill seemed annoyed by her enthusiasm and optimism about other people.

In time, both could see that their relationship was little more than a fantasy based on the film they were starring in when they met. Bette said Merrill wanted to believe that she was *All About Eve*'s Margo Channing while she thought he really was Bill Sampson, "this strong, protective, secure man." "We fell in love in the movies," Merrill said in a 1989 interview. "Subconsciously, we just went on after the movie was finished. As the demands of real life set in, we realized the premise was wrong."

Still, Bette refused to give up on what she considered to be her only true marriage. "For many years to come, I kept on hoping we could make it the marriage it had seemed to be in the beginning," she said later. "There was no question that we loved and respected each other. How could we fail?"

Bette's career was also in trouble. Good parts were hard to find, a development that mystified her but was – and remains today – a common problem for Hollywood actresses as their youth vanishes. After playing a bit role in a forgettable Gary Merrill movie, *Phone Call from a Stranger*, she accepted the lead in a film that seemed designed to exploit the themes of the hugely popular *All About Eve* and

*Sunset Boulevard* – but with far inferior results.

In the drama *The Star*, Bette played a once great, now fading Hollywood actress, Margaret Elliot, with no wealth left after spending it on her family and making three failed movies. In one memorable scene, she has auctioned off her property, returned to her apartment, and thrown her sister and brother-in-law out the door. Then she grasps her Academy Award and tells it, "Come on, Oscar, let's you and me get drunk!"

Though *The Star* had potential and a few scenes that showed off Bette's talents nicely, it was a critical and commercial failure. Still, Bette received her ninth Academy Award nomination, a reassuring validation of her status in Hollywood. But she did not win. In fact, it had been fourteen years since her last Oscar, in 1938.

As her movie roles were drying up, Bette was approached about starring in a new Broadway musical revue built around her talents. It was an audacious idea, and she was intrigued. Bette had limited experience in live theater – and even that was more than two decades ago. But she had a famous name, a loyal following, and could probably fill seats.

The show, *Two's Company*, would be a series of comedy sketches - and song-and-dance routines with tunes by a team of all-star songwriters: music by Vernon Duke and lyrics by Ogden Nash and

Sammy Cahn. It would begin with an out-of-town tryout tour of Detroit, Pittsburgh, and Boston before opening on Broadway in December 1952.

Bette leaped at the chance. She was tired of California; her film career was going nowhere. In addition, this could be the perfect way to explore a permanent move to her beloved East Coast, where she and Merrill could raise their three children far from the glitzy madness of Hollywood. She also hoped a change of scenery would help her struggling marriage. So they packed up and moved across the country, renting a penthouse in Manhattan near the East River.

From the start, Bette had bad feelings about the show – the material seemed uninspiring – but she chalked that up to being away from the theater for too long. The day before the opening in Detroit, Bette was up rehearsing all night and then ran through the complete show the next afternoon. By the time the curtain came up, she was so exhausted – and rattled by the live audience – that she passed out during her very first number.

As the curtain fell, Merrill rushed onto the stage. When Bette was revived, she demanded to finish the show. The curtain came back up again. Bette looked out beyond the footlights and said, "Well, you can't say I didn't fall for you." The crowd roared.

The Detroit critics were kind, but the good feelings

didn't last. The show was panned in Pittsburgh and, when it reached Boston, was completely overhauled, with various writers and directors called in to try to salvage it.

By the time *Two's Company* reached New York, Bette was exhausted and terrified of going on stage with brand new material and hardly any rehearsal time. Sucking it up, she went on anyway. The audience was welcoming but the reviews, she said, "were bloodcurdling."

Her fans did not seem to mind the negative press. But as Bette played to full houses, she could not understand why she was always so tired. Neither could her doctors. Then one Saturday, she went to a dentist between shows complaining of an inflamed wisdom tooth. It turned out she had osteomyelitis of the jaw, which required immediate surgery.

In a long and difficult operation, the surgeon carefully made the incisions from the inside of her mouth to avoid leaving facial scars by operating from the outside. Merrill flew back from a shoot in California to be there.

Without their headlining star, the producers of *Two's Company* closed the show, losing $320,000 of their investment. The surgery was costly to Bette as well. She was in the hospital for six weeks, and her long rehabilitation would ultimately keep her out of the movies for three years.

When Bette felt well enough to leave New York, she and Merrill decided it was time to live out their dream of raising their children in Maine, a place they both remembered fondly from their own childhoods. In April of 1953, they arrived at an inn in Yarmouth and spent the summer house hunting.

Finally, in September, they found the perfect place on a lane lined with apple trees: a three-story white clapboard house right on the ocean in Cape Elizabeth, just outside of Portland. It had large picture windows that provided a breathtaking view of the water. "The porches, the stacked lobster pots, the open fires, the pond for skating in winter, the cove," Bette said later, "the everything made it the perfect home for a family to be happy in."

Six-year-old B.D. entered the first grade at a Waynflete, a private school in Portland. They hired a governess named Elsa Stokes for Margot, two-and-a-half, and Mike, nineteen months. "I felt finally like the downright, upright, four-square married lady - P.T.A. and all," Bette said later. She loved the idea that her children would be spared the trauma she experienced of being constantly uprooted while growing up. She got so carried away that she even scouted locations for B.D.'s wedding.

It took Bette two years before she completely recovered from the surgery. Meanwhile, Maine was the best form of therapy she could imagine. She loved playing house – managing the kids' schedules, cooking, cleaning, and fixing up their home while her husband was off working. She approached her new role, she said, "with as much enthusiasm and perfection as I would approach playing a part."

By a cruel twist of fate, however, just when Bette found domestic stability – and really enjoyed being a mother and wife – her husband decided he didn't care for that side of her. "I don't want you in the kitchen all the time," Merrill complained. "How can you keep your sanity working around the house fourteen hours a day? How clean can a place be?"

But Merrill, as it turns out, had fallen in love with Bette Davis the movie star. He almost didn't recognize this ordinary woman he found himself married to. In fact, he finally told her, he just didn't love her anymore. "This was certainly a switch," Bette said later. "My crime had usually been the fact I was always working. Why couldn't I be just a wife?"

Their marital problems, however, were put on the back burner when the behavior of Margot, now three years old, became increasingly worrisome: her temper tantrums, her lack of energy, her slow language development. Even seven-year-old B.D. noticed that she seemed different, once saying to a friend, "My sister has a broken head."

Bette and Merrill took Margot to Presbyterian

Hospital in New York. After a week of tests, they were given the news they dreaded hearing, even as they had suspected it: Margot had a mental disability – they called her "retarded" at the time – a condition probably caused by brain damage before her adoption – perhaps a result of her birth mother's alcoholism or drugs she may have taken. The girl's IQ was sixty, alarmingly low. She would need more specialized care than Bette and Stokes could possibly provide at home.

When a doctor suggested enrolling her in the Lochland School in upstate New York, which focused on helping children with developmental disabilities, Bette refused, crying hysterically at the thought of sending their little girl away. But after meeting the school's founder, she became convinced it was the best course of action.

"It was a bitter blow and an enormous heartbreak to Gary and me," Bette recalled later. "It was not fair to her to have to compete with normal children, and not fair to the normal children to have to cope daily with a retarded child who would often be violent in her frustrations to keep up with her brother and sister."

Bette later said the most difficult day was when she helped Margot into her sailor suit and explained how nice her new school was going to be. Merrill boarded a plane with Margot and took her to Lochland while Bette stayed home with B.D. and

Mike. Later, Merrill remembered the beautiful Victorian house, the bright green grass, and the view of the lake – a lovely and sad scene.

In her 1962 memoir, *The Lonely Life*, Bette wrote that Margot was happy at Lochland and learning to handle her disability better with each passing year. "She loves her Christmas and summer holidays with us," she wrote. "The three Merrill children have a wonderful time when she is at home. With a sense of our loss, we send her back to Lochland each time. But we know it is the way it has to be." For the time being, anyway. Figuring out the best way to care for Margot as she got older would become a continuing source of tension between Bette and Merrill.

With Margot gone, Merrill became increasingly resentful that "Bette's child" B.D. was doing fine while "his" daughter had to be sent away. When he was home, he was restless, irritable, and often drunk.

Mired in depression over Margot and with marital tensions boiling, Bette received what felt like a lifeline when 20th Century Fox asked her to play Queen Elizabeth in *The Virgin Queen*. She had fully recovered from her surgery, they needed the money, and she could see that her homemaker routine was turning her husband off. "I had high hopes that with my return to acting things would be once more as they had been," she said later.

But being an actress – convincing your audiences that imaginary situations are real – sometimes involves lying to yourself as well. Bette didn't care. Something had to change. Leaving Merrill in Maine to care for Mike, she returned to Hollywood with B.D. and their governess Stokes, once again full of hope.

# 14
# "THE LITTLE WOMAN NO LONGER EXISTS."

Bette was terrified when she showed up on the Hollywood set of *The Virgin Queen* in early 1955.

It had been three years since she had performed in front of the camera's unforgiving lens – and sixteen years since she had first played the monarch as a younger woman in *The Private Lives of Elizabeth and Essex*. But as soon as she spoke her first lines – "Mistress Throckmorton, is this your pet swine? I see you cast pearls before him." - Bette relaxed and found her rhythm.

Curtis Bernhardt, who had directed her in two earlier films, had urged *The Virgin Queen* director Henry Koster to reconsider working with Bette - she will drive you nuts, Bernhardt warned. So when Bette had Koster over for tea before filming started, the director made it clear that if she was going to make his life miserable, he was out. She chuckled and told him that if he knew what he was doing, all would be well. The chat seemed to help. Bette behaved herself, and throughout the filming, they got along like old friends.

As Bette began playing the forty-eight-year-old Queen Elizabeth, she was about a month shy of her own forty-seventh birthday. As in her previous portrayal of the queen, she shaved her head and eyebrows to look the part in this dramatic tale of Elizabeth's unreturned affection for explorer Walter Raleigh, played by the British actor Richard Todd.

(During production, Bette's son Mike finally got to come see his mom at work and observe a movie set for the first time. He watched with his dad as Bette, while filming a scene as the queen, shouted angrily at her co-star Todd. In a sign of how bitter his parents' marriage had become, Mike listened for a bit and then asked his dad, "Why is Mummy yelling at that man instead of you?")

The movie premiered in Portland, Maine, on July 22, 1955, and raised money for the Portland Children's Theatre. Newspaper tycoon Jean Gannett hosted an afternoon clambake, followed by cocktails at Bette and Merrill's home and a buffet dinner at the Eastland Hotel. About 10,000 people showed up at the Strand Theatre, overwhelming the capacity of the 2,000-seat theater and creating a mob scene.

The critics agreed that Bette gave an astute, albeit subtle performance – and praised her courage for revisiting a character she had played so well in 1939. "She makes Elizabeth a strident, domineering, piteous queen," wrote Bosley Crowther in *The New York Times*. "She is now a little stronger and a little more freakish than before." For some reviewers, the only distraction was the way she chose to walk: One wrote that she resembled Groucho Marx; another said she ambled around like a horse jockey.

Clearly, Bette Davis was a force to be reckoned with once again. In March of that year, she had been asked to present the Best Actor award at the Oscar ceremony. She arrived in full Elizabethan dress, with a cap covering her still-shaven head. Before presenting the trophy - to Marlon Brando for *On the Waterfront* - she was terribly nervous about how she would be greeted after her three-year absence. She needn't have worried. The ovation she received, Bette said later, was one of the greatest moments of her life. Turns out she really *had* been missed after all.

Despite that temporary high, Bette was not overjoyed to be the toast of Hollywood once again. Motherhood had changed her. "My real happiness was at home with the children," she said later. When all the film publicity was over, she was ecstatic to return to Maine for the rest of the summer, the most beautiful time of year on her beloved rocky coast.

At summer's end, it was difficult to say goodbye to her children and head back to California. But she was not in a financial position to turn down work and was grateful to be offered a part in a new Columbia film, *Storm Center*, as a librarian who refused to ban a book about communism. A liberal Democrat with a lifelong fondness for books, Bette was happy to be making a political statement by participating in the first overtly anti-McCarthyism film Hollywood had ever produced.

But *Storm Center* did not do well at the box-office when it was released in July of 1956. While the critics congratulated the filmmakers for tackling such a worthy, controversial subject, most felt the results were uninspiring. (*Time Out London* called it "didactic, laborious.") Bette received generally positive reviews, however, with *The New York Times* commending her "fearless and forceful performance."

When another opportunity came up right away – MGM's family drama *The Catered Affair*, based on a teleplay by Paddy Chayefsky – Merrill and the children came to California for Thanksgiving and stayed with her during filming. But the movie bombed when it came out the following summer, eviscerated by reviewers and losing over $100,000 (almost $1 million today).

With her career in a nosedive, Bette's marriage provided no safe haven. When shooting of *The Catered Affair* was completed, Merrill suggested that he and Bette take a holiday together, hoping it might give their faltering marriage a boost. So they hopped in a new car they had just bought – a Mercedes 190 SL – and drove to Florida, where they chartered a schooner for two weeks. But there was no escaping their problems, no matter how exotic the location: In the end, Merrill had simply fallen out of love with Bette, and there really wasn't anything either of them could do about it. By the time they rejoined their children in Maine a month later, they were further apart than ever.

"We," Bette said, "had had it."

Still, Bette clung to the hope that the marriage could be salvaged - that somehow, the magic between them might return. So she suggested that the whole family move back to California. Maybe having everyone together in one place, she reasoned – without Dad and Mom always flying off to make a movie – would create more domestic stability. At the very least, it might rehabilitate their fading careers.

Bette was tired of cranking out forgettable films while Merrill was mired in supporting roles in lackluster Westerns, war movies, and medical dramas. So Bette and Merrill sold their dream home on the Maine coast, rented a house in Los Angeles, and hoped for the best.

On a losing streak with her films, Bette focused on being a wife and mother – "the kitchen my domain" she said – and accepted her first role in the popular new medium, television, in 1956. She would appear on no fewer than eight television programs in 1957 and 1958 (both years when no Bette Davis big-screen films were released), mostly episodes in anthology series sponsored by big corporations such as Schlitz, Ford, and General Electric that were sprouting up in those early days of television. To many, it appeared that her big-screen career was over.

Accustomed to a high style of living, but with no big studio checks coming in, Bette and Merrill fell into debt. Instead of investing her money, she lavished her family and friends with gifts – and for many years supported Ruthie and Bobby. Merrill was also bad at managing his funds. One year, the IRS informed him that he owed $50,000 in back taxes. When Bette's agent, Jules Stein, offered to manage the family's finances, she icily told him to stick to finding her jobs.

The consequences of their spendthrift ways were humiliating. Almost daily, a bill collector would show up at their door, often a shy young man who would lower his head and say, "I hate to do this to you . . . "Ever proud and defiant, Bette would stoically accept the invoice and say, "Quite all right."

As her life spiraled downward, professionally and personally, Bette drank more than usual, which intensified her typical belligerence.

The producer William Frye recalled going out to dinner one night with Bette, Merrill, and the director Herschel Daugherty and his wife. After a few cocktails, Daugherty, just drunk enough to forget his manners, pointed at Bette while emphasizing something he was saying. She flew into a rage. "Don't you *dare* put your finger in my face!" she screamed. The room fell quiet. Even the piano player stopped.

Herschel tried to apologize, but Bette would not have it, yelling that she never wanted to see him again. The other diners watched, riveted by this live Bette Davis performance. Disgusted by her behavior, Merrill left, muttering, "I've had it." Herschel and his wife escaped, too, but Bette didn't move. "Cleaned this place out pretty good, didn't I?" she said with a bitter smile. "Now let's go someplace!" She and Frye got up and headed to Mocambo, a celebrity hangout on the Sunset Strip.

Merrill was also a drinker and often found himself sending roses to whatever nightclub employee he had insulted the night before. When both were drunk, their fights were legendary, and the animosity lingered. For Merrill's birthday one August, she put together a surprise party for him. But instead of a traditional cake, she got an artificial one with icing on it. And instead of having the words "Happy Birthday" scrawled across it, the fake cake said, "Fuck You."

In June of 1957, Bette finally filed a separation action in Santa Monica Superior Court. On her behalf, attorney David Tannenbaum charged that Merrill was guilty of "extreme cruelty" which was causing Bette "grievous mental suffering." She asked for custody of the kids and financial support for them and herself.

"I think Gary and I were very much in love when we married," Bette said later. "Once the love bug wears off, as it inevitably does, you are shocked to discover that you really didn't know the object of your affections at all."

As her marriage imploded, Bette got an exciting career jolt when she was offered a role in a stage play in Los Angeles based on the novel *Look Homeward, Angel* by Thomas Wolfe, appearing alongside Anthony Perkins. But nothing seemed to go right during this wrenching period of her life. As she was moving into a new house on Bundy Drive in the Brentwood neighborhood, she opened a door and stepped into what she thought was a closet. It was the basement door, and she tumbled down the stairs and broke her back.

Bette was hospitalized for four months, forcing her to give up the play and also cancel a high-profile TV appearance on Lucille Ball's *Lucy and Desi Comedy Hour*. While she was recuperating, she stayed with Bobby in Laguna Beach for a while. (Later, she sued for damages, and the jury awarded her $65,700.)

In early 1958, when she was well enough to work again, Bette went back to television, the only job offers coming her way. One gig was courtesy of William Frye, who had created a one-hour special just for her, *Fraction of a Second* (based on a short story by Daphne du Maurier called *Split Second*). Rehearsals were going well until Frye got a call from Bette at 5:00 a.m. on the first day of shooting.

"You're going to have to get somebody else for the part," Bette said. "There's no way I can do the picture."

"Bette, you're due at the studio in an hour for makeup," Frye cried. "You *have* to do this picture."

"Well, I won't be there. I'm not feeling well. I'm sick."

After much back-and-forth, Frye agreed to postpone filming her parts for one day, but sent a doctor over to see what was wrong with her. Later that morning, the doctor called Frye to report that Bette wasn't sick; she and Merrill had had a nasty fight the night before that ended up with Bette falling – or being pushed – face first into her gravel driveway.

One side of her face as so badly bruised and scratched, in fact, that she could not be filmed on that side. The next day, they shot her from the other side; finally, on the third day, heavy makeup was enough to hide the damage.

But soon there would be more turmoil on the set. Bette clashed with Frye again, this time over a scene she insisted on filming with her back to the camera. When he demanded that her face be visible, she screamed, "*Goddamn it,* I was *acting* before you were even *thought* of!"

When Bette lost that battle, she refused to talk to Frye until the last day of filming - April 5, 1958, which happened to be her fiftieth birthday. "Where's that producer who thinks he knows everything?" Bette yelled in her dressing room after shooting had wrapped. "Tell him to get his ass into my room for a drink!"

Their friendship re-established, Frye was saddened to realize that Bette had no plans for her birthday. So he scrambled to assemble a last-minute party at his house in Coldwater Canyon and invited the cast and crew. In the roller-coaster world of Bette Davis, her spirits were suddenly high once more. "It was one of the best nights the house ever saw," Frye said later, "full of fun and laughter."

After twenty-seven years in a business that always seemed to favor commerce over art, Bette had become cynical enough to view most of her film offers as excuses to make money – and perhaps even get some all-expenses-paid foreign travel. In May, she accepted a $50,000 offer from producer Sam Bronston for a small role as the Russian Empress Catherine the Great in the film *John Paul Jones*, about America's revolutionary war hero. It was an easy payday – $425,000 in today's dollars – for a four-day job that included a trip to the shooting location of Madrid, Spain. She wasted little time climbing aboard the SS *Independence* with her guests Bobby and B.D., who had just turned eleven.

The film itself wasn't much when it finally came out, but she got an excellent vacation in Europe out of the deal. When the shoot was over, Bette and her entourage – which included Bobby, B.D., and William Frye - went to Rome. There, they visited the Pantheon and Coliseum, the famous film studio Cinecittà to watch a chariot race being shot for William Wyler's Ben-Hur. They also had dinner with the Italian actress Anna Magnani, before moving on to Venice and Milan.

From Italy, Bette flew to London, where she had another job waiting, a British thriller called *The Scapegoat*. Again, it was a supporting role, this time as a domineering, eccentric countess. During the filming, she came to dislike her co-star, Alec

Guinness – she complained that he gave her few facial reactions to work with – while Guinness said he found Bette cold and remote and was convinced that she never really understood her character.

*The Scapegoat* was yet another dud when it came out in August of 1959. It had been a rough decade for Bette, who hadn't had a hit movie since *All About Eve* nine years before, and critics were blasting her for caring more about showing off than creating compelling characters. "The criterion for her choice of film would appear to be that nothing must compete with the full display of each facet of the Davis art," wrote the London critic Richard Winninger. "Only bad films are good enough for her."

Fortunately, Bette was still being considered for theater roles – but her traumatic personal life would follow her even to the sanctuary of the stage. The writer and director Norman Corwin approached her in 1959 with an audacious idea: performing in a show called *The World of Carl Sandburg* - a collection of Sandburg poems in a play format, which would tour the country in a series of one-night stands. If that didn't sound risky enough, Corwin threw in another wrinkle: She wanted Bette to co-star with her husband.

It came as a surprise to many who knew them that Bette and Merrill both accepted. Their decision was largely based on the longshot hope that it might, somehow, save their marriage. Merrill was the more gung-ho about the idea when they packed up and headed to Maine, where rehearsals would begin before the show opened in Portland. But being under two contracts with Bette – as husband and co-star – proved too much for Merrill. By the time rehearsals started, they had separated again.

"Security was always bad medicine for him," Bette said. "Once he had something, I'm afraid, he didn't want it any more."

It was an unbearably awkward situation – a bitterly estranged husband and wife working together – but the contracts had been signed, and there was nothing anybody could do about it. So with B.D. and Michael attending a boarding school in California – and Bobby living near them to help out – Bette and Merrill were on the other side of the country trying to get through rehearsals without killing each other.

When *The World of Carl Sandburg* finally opened on October 12, 1959, Maine's U.S. Senator Edmund Muskie and the poet Sandburg himself showed up. It was a true test of Bette and Merrill's acting abilities to pretend to be a happily married couple on stage. Somehow, they pulled it off. Reviews were glowing, and the show embarked on its tour of thirty-two U.S. cities - including Bette's hometown of Lowell, Massachusetts - which continued into the following year. Career-wise it was a godsend for Bette. With her movie career stalled and possibly over, she had an acclaimed, profitable outlet for her creative energies.

But the biggest test of the show was yet to come. When they finally reached Los Angeles, Bette was terrified, bracing for the worst. "Hollywood perversely wants you to fail," she said later. Still famous but not the movie mega-star she once was, Bette imagined her enemies gobbling up tickets just to see how low she had fallen.

But with Ruthie in the front row – for the last time, as it turned out – Bette received thunderous applause when she made her entrance. The ovation was deafening again when the curtains came down at the end. It was a hit. Their one-week engagement turned into four.

When the company reached San Francisco, the tour was over - and so was Bette's marriage. It had been nearly ten years since she met Merrill, in the same city, while filming *All About Eve*. In her memoir, Bette offered no details about the final, knock-down, drag-out fight that did them in except to say, "The last explosion could have been heard round the world. There was no longer any point in even trying."

Bette filed for divorce and served her husband the papers. Their separation agreement guaranteed Merrill visitation rights with the children but forbade him from continuing to perform in *The*

*World of Carl Sandburg* in New York, where it was scheduled to open in the fall. He was replaced by the actor Leif Erickson.

*The World of Carl Sandburg* ran for only twenty-nine performances in New York, closing on October 8, 1960 – perhaps because it had lost the prurient interest in seeing Bette's volatile marriage on display. For his part, Merrill said he never regretted being part of the show, calling it a high point in his career.

Later, Bette would admit that she deserved her share of the blame for the failure of her fourth marriage, the closest she ever came to a workable union. "I am sure I have been uncompromising, peppery, intractable, monomaniacal, tactless, volatile and oft-times disagreeable," she said. "I stand accused of it all." But she also realized that it was never her fate to become a housewife who finds domestic happiness. "It was the wrong casting," she said later. "Actors can't expect life to be this bucolic."

Or perhaps it was just bad timing. After devoting her youth to her career, she wondered if she simply waited too long to commit to a husband and family – and then gave herself to a man she could not, ultimately, depend upon. "I admit that Gary broke my heart," she said. "He killed the dream forever. The little woman no longer exists."

When *The World of Carl Sandburg* closed, Bette stayed in New York, where she had brought her children to live. She got a tutor for B.D. and enrolled her in a riding academy while Mike went to a private school for boys. Joined by the family's dachshund, French poodle, and Siamese cat, Bette at age fifty-two decided it was time to do what many celebrities eventually get around to doing as a way to make some money, settle old scores, and burnish their legacies: write her memoir, which she would title *The Lonely Life*.

She also began looking for acting work and found it with *Pocketful of Miracles*, a Frank Capra remake of his own 1933 comedy-drama, *Lady for a Day*, based on a Damon Runyon short story. Bette's role of Apple Annie – a homeless woman given the chance to be a wealthy woman for a day – had already been turned down by Katharine Hepburn, Helen Hayes, Jean Arthur, and Shirley Booth. Still struggling financially, Bette could not be quite so picky, since the job came with a $100,000 payday ($800,000 today).

True to form, Bette clashed repeatedly with her co-star, Glenn Ford, who had enraged her by giving an interview suggesting that he was the one who got her the job as a favor, to revive her flagging career. Their battles during the shooting in the spring and early summer of 1961 gave Capra headaches so bad that, at one point, he became incapacitated. When it was released in December, the film was generally panned. (*Films in Review*'s Elaine Rothschild dismissed it as "unbelievable and unfunny.")

But Bette was about to suffer another blow far worse than making another bad film, or even losing another husband. As filming was wrapping up, Ruthie, who had been ill since Christmas, took a turn for the worse.

Bobby had been taking care of her at Ruthie's home in Laguna Beach, and Bette visited whenever she could. An inveterate planner all her life, Ruthie told anyone who would listen that she was now planning to die. "She was seventy-six," Bette said later, "and that bursting heart was exhausted." "I'm tired, Bette!" Ruthie would wail, and proceed to explain how she wanted her possessions divided. "I'm tired darling . . . tired of the fight."

Her mother was not kidding. On the morning of July 1, 1961, fifty-three years to the day after she married Bette's father, Ruth Augusta Davis went to sleep and never woke up.

"Bobby and I were speechless," Bette recalled later. "We wanted to hide in the bathroom as we used to do when we shared any grief. It seemed impossible. We felt like orphans. Her vitality, her joy, were gone forever. Her protection and her dependency, her wisdom and her little-girlness and her guts."

Bette's life with her mother flashed before her eyes. Ruthie sitting in the window of the photography shop in Norwalk, Connecticut, hunched over negatives for hours while Bette tried to launch her acting career; marching into John Murray Anderson's drama school and demanding a spot for her daughter, even though she was broke; shopping at discount stores for cute little knickknacks to decorate their drab little apartments; filling Bette's homes with the flowers Ruthie loved.

"She was made up of so many things, my mother," Bette said later. "Brutal honesty and silly deceits; self-indulgence and endless sacrifices; love and loyalty and that abundance of joy of living. She was so many things - a rounded woman, not a washed-out stereotype. Ruthie! Without whom."

In her grief, Bette became wracked with guilt about the anger and frustration she often felt toward her mother – for Ruthie's constant intrusions into her private life, her mother's resistance to Bette's attempts to grow up and become independent, her extravagant spending of her daughter's money. In her anger, she forgot that without Ruthie, there would be no Bette Davis the Movie Star; no huge paychecks and luxury homes; no adoring fans. Bette immediately began revising the chapters of her book that were critical of her mother. "How dared I expect perfection in so magnificent a creature?" she wrote in *The Lonely Life*.

Suddenly, nothing mattered to Bette – the inconsequential film she had just completed, the exciting new Tennessee Williams play, *Night of the*

*Iguana*, that Williams himself had asked her to do. None of it mattered. Freshly divorced, and now facing life without her mom, Bette felt more alone than ever. Just like Ruthie, in fact, when Bette was a little girl.

“I am exactly where Mother was at the beginning,” she said later. “Alone with my children - alone against the world.”

# 15

# "THE POSSIBILITY OF STARS IN TEMPERAMENTAL COLLISION HAS THE APPEAL OF GLADIATORIAL COMBAT FOR THE TRIBE OF CALIGULA."

After she buried her mother, Bette felt desolate. Her children were off at boarding schools because she didn't want to use them as an emotional crutch while she grieved.

Fortunately, she had work to keep her busy – a role in the new Tennessee Williams play, *Night of the Iguana*, scheduled to open on Broadway in December of 1961. She had met the great playwright the year before while touring Florida with *The World of Carl Sandburg*. Williams wanted to gauge her interest in playing Maxine Faulk, the recently widowed manager of the play's low-end Acapulco hotel.

"It was certainly the tertiary part," Bette said, "but

as I have said many times since, I would rather have the third part in a Tennessee Williams play than a lead in an ordinary play."

When opening night arrived, however, Bette was haunted by memories. Not only of Ruthie but of her past in Rochester, New York, where *The Night of the Iguana* was beginning its out-of-town tryout. It was in Rochester, after all, that she had gotten her start, at age twenty, with a bit part in George Cukor's theater company. The memories came rushing back – Ruthie advising her to learn the role of Pearl because she somehow knew that the actress playing her would have an accident. Bette choked up remembering her train trip to Rochester, the first time she had been separated from her mom.

Now, with Ruthie's death, their final separation was complete. It was Bette's first stage performance without her mom, who had always sent her a telegram saying, "Remember, darling – I'm in the front row" – even when she couldn't make it. This time, there was no telegram.

But as Bette stood backstage, nervously waiting for the curtain to go up, she had a vision: "Mother was there," she said later. "I saw her, back at Cushing when I graduated, smiling gaily in that old flowered hat that was supposed to hide her developer-poisoned face. I saw her sitting there, spunky and proud."

At that moment, Bette realized she could not let her mother down. Her cue came. She strode on stage. "Shannon!" she said, as Maxine Faulk. "Hi Baby — I've been expecting you here."

Though *The Night of the Iguana* is now considered by many to be the last of the great Tennessee Williams plays, some critics at the time were not impressed. During the tour, *Time* magazine, noting that iguanas are Mexico's equivalent to the American Thanksgiving Day turkey, said that despite impressive performances by Margaret Leighton and Bette Davis, the play itself "is indeed a massive turkey." In Chicago, the Tribune described the show as "bleakly dull."

Compounding the show's troubles was Bette's return to form as malcontent. Her mother's death had not mellowed her.

Case in point: As the tour progressed, Williams told Bette that her portrayal of Maxine had moments of greatness. But, overall, she wasn't getting the character right. In Chicago, he sent her a note saying Maxine should be more free-spirited, like the ocean, with loose hair instead of the tidy wig Bette was wearing. By then, Bette seemed to be fed up. She refused to listen to director Frank Corsaro and insisted that he stay out of the theater building. In his *Memoirs*, Williams said that Corsaro did indeed stay out, but remained in Chicago. Bette protested, diva-like, because it made her ill at ease knowing he was nearby. She yelled that he should go back to New York and the damn Actors Studio that shaped him. Williams himself, with the help of others, stepped in to direct.

Maybe Bette was right. Another Broadway director, Josh Logan, saw *The Night of the Iguana* when it opened on Broadway at the Royale Theatre. He liked the show and said Bette was fantastic, with just the right amount of humor and tawdriness. Indeed, Chicago critics aside, the show was a success in the Big Apple, with audiences drawn to the theater largely because of Bette's star power.

Still, it wasn't long before Bette started calling off performances. Since her character is offstage for much of the play, Bette was bitter about how little she had to do, according to Williams' agent Audrey Wood.

In April of 1962, after four months, Bette finally quit the show, replaced by Shelley Winters. When she first entered her dressing room, Winters saw that Bette had left her a note, written in lipstick on the mirror. It warned her that it would take only a couple of performances to understand why Bette quit.

It actually took Winters three performances to figure it out. Maxine Faulk was conceived as a comic role to relieve the more depressing aspects of the story, but many of her funniest lines were ruined when the actors Margaret Leighton and Patrick O'Neal deliberately distracted the audience's attention to themselves. Without Bette, the show struggled on for a while longer and then closed after 316 performances.

As she struggled in *The Night of the Iguana* and grieved over her mother's death, Bette felt like she was stuck in a rut, both professionally and personally. She had certainly lost whatever optimism she used to possess about finding domestic happiness. Her divorce from Merrill, she said, was the last straw that "convinces me I am obviously a complete failure as a wife."

Meanwhile, she was fighting custody battles over Michael, now ten years old. The situation was complicated by the fact that Merrill, after his divorce from Bette, had begun seeing Rita Hayworth (the former pin-up girl, now in her forties, had been married five times by then). This drove Bette into fits of fury. One day, Merrill said, he and Hayworth took his kids and her kids to a stage production of *The Sound of Music*. Afterward, as he dropped B.D. and Mike off at Bette's home, she leaned out an upstairs window and screamed profanities, calling Hayworth a whore who was not fit to be anywhere near her children.

The next day, Bette met with her attorneys to try to revoke all visitation rights from her ex-husband. She succeeded, but after some time passed, a judge gave

Merrill the right to see Mike every other weekend and during half of his school vacation. Angry, Bette hurled another grenade by sending her son to live full-time with his father, knowing Merrill had trouble with the rigors of parenthood. But before the school year was over, she reconsidered and took Michael back into her custody.

How Michael came out of this relatively unscathed is a minor miracle.

Ghostwriter Sandford Dody, who helped Bette with *The Lonely Life*, said that Michael was good natured, but kept to himself - and seemed to have a lot of wisdom for a young boy. When his father was away, Bette would roughhouse with her son like his Dad used to, Dody said. But Mike seemed cautious, knowing that his mother could switch from playful to temperamental suddenly, without warning.

Merrill, using hip 1960s vernacular, would later describe Mike as "square," especially compared to his own bohemian lifestyle. Despite Mike's turbulent childhood – constantly moving between California, Maine, and New York – the boy held it together and grew up to become a successful attorney.

As Bette's personal and professional life was unraveling, her career got an unexpected boost from an unlikely source – her old nemesis Joan Crawford. While she was still appearing in *The Night of the Iguana*, Bette got a backstage visit from Crawford, who suggested they make a film together. The two had not reconciled after their earlier spats, and in fact barely knew one another, having worked at different Hollywood studios for most of their careers. But they had some important things in common. Both had once been huge stars, and now, in their fifties, neither one was in great demand. Crawford's idea was that they should let bygones be bygones and team up on this new film that could help revive both of their careers. Seeing her logic – and needing the work – Bette agreed. Based on a suspense novel by Henry Farrell, the film was called *What Ever Happened to Baby Jane?*

Crawford had sent the novel to Robert Aldrich, the director of the film-noir classic *Kiss Me Deadly* who would later make *The Dirty Dozen* and *The Longest Yard.* Aldrich loved the book, bought the rights, and agreed that Bette and Crawford would be perfect for the leading roles of aging sisters, both former movie stars, who live together in a hellish existence.

A few weeks later, Aldrich flew to New York and met Bette at her townhouse on Seventy-eighth Street. First, Bette wanted assurance that she would get the part she wanted – the Baby Jane of the title. Aldrich agreed.

Then she brought up a sensitive matter: Crawford was well-known for having affairs with her directors, which gave her an inordinate amount of power on the set. Since Aldrich had previously directed Crawford, Bette had a question: "Mr. Aldrich, have you had any, uh, personal relationship with Miss Crawford?"

In the awkward moment that followed, Bette added that her concern was that she be treated fairly. Aldrich laughed and said he understood. "The answer is no," he replied, "not that I didn't have the opportunity."

With sexual politics out of the way and his two stars on board, Aldrich turned to fund-raising. But few producers or investors wanted to gamble on two older female stars from a bygone era. Even Warner Brothers, Bette's studio for so many years, turned him down. "Recast it," one producer told Aldrich. "Get some box-office names, and we'll give you whatever you want. But we won't give you a dime for those two old broads."

It was a difficult time for actresses. While women ruled the big screen in the thirties and forties, and films were often made with a female audience in mind, that all changed in the fifties. In those postwar years, war movies evolved into a lasting trend of films with male-dominated themes, and the biggest stars, from Marlon Brando to Jimmy Stewart, tended to be men.

Despite those headwinds, Aldrich finally found his funding. Eliot Hyman, head of Seven Arts Productions – who knew something about horror shows, having financed *The Curse of Frankenstein* in 1957 – could see the potential in this strange film of two aging sisters driving each other mad; it might even attract fans of *Psycho*, a big hit for Alfred Hitchcock two years earlier. With a small budget of less than $1 million ($8 million today), the movie would be shot within a month. Bette and Crawford agreed to relatively low salaries of $50,000 each ($400,000 now) in exchange for a percentage of profits.

As the project moved ahead, the next challenge was overcoming the antagonistic history of the film's two stars, which had lasted some seventeen years.

In her second memoir, *This 'N That*, Bette tried to take the high road when discussing Crawford, as if trying to show that she was a consummate professional who could do her job despite the fraught history she had with her co-star. "I admired the strength and ambition that propelled her in spite of her background," Bette wrote. But the attempt to be gracious was a backhanded compliment at best since in the next breath she mentioned that Crawford's father had run off with a stripper from a Galveston waterfront bar, leaving behind his wife and two children.

Bette was well aware that Hollywood considered the frosty Davis-Crawford relationship to be perhaps its most epic and fascinating feud. "*Feud* is a Hollywood word, a wildly overused Hollywood word," Bette wrote, attempting to set the record straight. "Did Bette Davis and Joan Crawford ever feud during the filming of *Baby Jane*? No!" (More than half a century later, however, a 2017 television miniseries about the making of *Baby Jane*, called *Feud*, would thrill new generations of viewers eager to see Susan Sarandon, as Bette, and Jessica Lange, as Crawford, tear each other to shreds.)

Even at the time, Hollywood was abuzz with gossip about the filming. In a July 1962 article entitled "Hollywood T.N.T.," Murray Schumach of *The New York Times* wrote, "the possibility of stars in temperamental collision has the appeal of gladiatorial combat for the tribe of Caligula."

Part of the appeal of the rivalry was the perception that, as actresses, Bette and Crawford were polar opposites. Bette was never considered a beauty queen but saw herself a consummate artist; at her best, the critics agreed. Crawford, on the other hand, was viewed as a glamourous pin-up girl with limited range whose success, both on screen and off, had much to do with her sex appeal. Those stereotypes, however, did not withstand deeper scrutiny. Bette could be sexy when she wanted to be and turned in many awful performances. Crawford, meanwhile, could, at times, be a better actress than she was given credit for, showing it in films like 1945's *Mildred Pierce*, for which she won a Best Actress Oscar.

Clearly, Bette's reputation as a better actress rankled Crawford. "I don't hate Bette Davis, even though the press want me to," Crawford later told the author Roy Newquist in his book, *Conversations with Joan Crawford.* "I resent her. I don't see how she built a career out of a set of mannerisms instead of real acting ability. Take away the pop-eyes, the cigarette, and those funny clipped words, and what have you got? She's phony, but I guess the public likes that."

Even their approaches to preparing for their roles was starkly different. While Bette seemed to take an almost perverse enjoyment out of looking as awful as possible in many of her movies, Crawford always seemed to be primping, regardless of which character she was playing.

Those tendencies showed up in *Baby Jane* as well. Bette insisted on doing her own makeup - partly because her vision of Jane Hudson was so frightening that she didn't think any professional makeup artist would be willing to go as far as she wanted. Bette's idea was that Jane never washed her face and merely added another layer of makeup every day. So she used a chalk-white base, with lots of eye shadow, and a bleached blond wig with curls that showed that her pathetic, aging character still wanted to look like a baby doll. One makeup artist told her that if he ever made her up that way, he would never work in Hollywood again.

A few days after shooting started, Aldrich said to

Bette, "You can't wear this makeup. It's too much. It's laughable." After seeing the rushes, however, Bette was more convinced than ever that she was right. She threatened to leave the production if she were forced to change her makeup. By the end of the week, he was sold.

The producers of *Baby Jane* were having the opposite problem with Crawford, who wanted to look as pretty as possible despite playing a woman in a wheelchair who had been wasting away at home for twenty years. She wanted coiffed hair, beautiful gowns, and polished fingernails. Aldrich eventually convinced his star to adopt a plainer appearance, but one day he spent an entire morning trying to get her to remove her nail polish for a scene that showed off her hands.

"You have taken everything else away from me," Crawford wailed. "You're not taking away my nail polish!"

As shooting progressed, the tension between the stars was evident. When Crawford, whose fourth husband was the chairman of the board of Pepsi, brought a cooler of Pepsi for the cast and crew, Bette brought a cooler of Coke (she also claimed that Crawford was constantly drinking her Pepsi spiked with vodka). When Crawford asked Bette to sign a copy of her memoir, *The Lonely Life*, Bette snidely scrawled the words, "Joan, Thanks for wanting my autograph. Bette."

Every day, Crawford sent Bette a rose anonymously and later insisted that her motives were pure. "I thought we should be friends," she said. But Bette was appalled when she learned who they were from. Some have even speculated that Crawford, who was rumored to be bisexual, was making romantic advances that were being rebuffed by the firmly heterosexual Bette.

"I believed her attempts to butter me up were absolutely insincere," Bette said later. "I hated it when she would send me flowers or little gifts, or gooey notes on that baby blue notepaper of hers." She added that Crawford "carried this saccharine politeness to such an exaggerated degree of courtesy that it was disgusting and irritating."

With the press hyping their feud, *What Ever Happened to Baby Jane?* was an enormous hit when it opened in New York theaters on Halloween of 1962. In just the first weekend, it brought in $1.6 million and became profitable in less than two weeks. Costing under $1.1 million to make, the film ended up grossing $9.5 million.

Even with such success, Crawford could not resist saying nasty things about her co-star. "Sure, she stole most of my big scenes," she told an interviewer, "but the funny thing is, when I see it again, she stole them because she looked a parody of herself and I still looked like a star . . . she tried too hard."

As the years went by, Crawford noted, the film became a favorite of drag queens and Bette Davis impersonators. "I never wanted to be some sort of joke," she said, "and thank God, I haven't been."

Things got uglier when Bette was nominated for an Oscar for her performance, but Crawford was not. Bette became convinced that Crawford began actively campaigning among Academy voters to deny her the enormous honor of becoming the first actress ever to win three Best Actress statuettes. Determined to upstage her rival on the night of the awards, Crawford also contacted the other nominees and offered to accept their Oscars if they won and were unable to attend.

In those days, the nominees sat in separate dressing rooms backstage and watched the event on a TV monitor. Watching with her friend, the producer Bill Frye, Bette was sure she would win. But when the actor Maximilian Schell announced the winner, she was stunned to hear him say Anne Bancroft's name, for the Helen Keller story, *The Miracle Worker*.

Sure enough, Crawford soon swept on stage to accept the trophy for Bancroft, who was in New York performing in a play. She looked dazzling, in a beaded silver sheath accented with caviar pearls and diamonds. But first, she breezed past Bette's dressing-room door. "I will never forget the look she gave me," Bette said. "It was triumphant. The look clearly said, you didn't win and I am elated!"

As Crawford took the stage, she received a standing ovation. Holding the Oscar trophy next to Best Actor Gregory Peck, who won for *To Kill a Mockingbird*, she basked in the applause. That was too much for Bette. She turned to Frye and said, in a loud voice, "Let's get *out* of here!"

Bette stormed out of the Santa Monica Civic Auditorium saying she was going home, but Frye convinced her to attend the after-party at the Beverly Hilton so she wouldn't look like a sore loser. There, they were joined by B.D., Bobby, Olivia de Havilland, and Aldrich and his wife. At their table, Bette grabbed a glass, filled it with scotch, and said, "This is for La Belle Crawford."

"She doesn't drink scotch," Frye said. "She drinks vodka."

"I don't care *what* she *drinks*," Bette fumed. "This is going into her *fucking face.*"

When Crawford entered the ballroom with her usual regal air, Bette thought better of dousing her with scotch. But she did demand that her group leave immediately. Later, as they sat around Bette's kitchen drinking, de Havilland lamented how terrible it was that Bette had lost and Crawford had stolen the show. Now everybody who sees a picture of her holding Bancroft's Oscar will assume she won, de Havilland said.

"Well, you have to admit," Frye said, "when Crawford came out on that stage, with that dress and that array of diamonds, she did look like the movie star of all time."

Everyone stopped talking. Dead silence. Later, Frye said it was the most inappropriate comment he had ever made in his life – "the wrong thing at the wrong time in front of the wrong person."

"What did you say?" Bette said. Mortified, Frye said nothing. She approached him with a large knife. Until that moment, she had been slicing bread to make toast and scrambled eggs for her guests. Now she seemed intent on using the knife for another purpose. She pressed it to Frye's chest, and repeated, "What did you say?"

Sitting in his chair, frozen with fright, Frye imagined his own blood staining his nice dress shirt. Then he bravely – or perhaps stupidly – repeated what he had said. Another silence. As the guests held their breath, they would have been forgiven for wondering how much acting had been involved in the violent sociopaths Bette has portrayed over the years. Finally, she pulled the knife away. "You make me *sick*," she said, spitting out the words. Then she went back to slicing bread. The party continued until 5:00 a.m.

Without a doubt, *What Ever Happened to Baby Jane*? was one of the strangest comebacks in

Hollywood history. But make no mistake: Bette Davis had returned.

# 16

# "MOTHER OF THREE. DIVORCEE. AMERICAN. THIRTY YEARS EXPERIENCE AS AN ACTRESS. WANTS STEADY EMPLOYMENT IN HOLLYWOOD."

During Bette's war with Joan Crawford, she mentioned how silly it was for her rival to sabotage her chances of winning the Best Actress Oscar in 1963. After all, the trophy normally adds at least $1 million to a film's ticket sales - and, as Bette noted – both actresses were getting a percentage of the profits. In other words, an Oscar for Bette would have meant a financial windfall for Crawford.

Despite the ego and pride war, both actresses cashed in: *What Ever Happened to Baby Jane?* was a runaway success. Bette went from struggling has-been actress to a reborn star with homes in the tony Bel Air section of Los Angeles and Westport, Connecticut.

When shooting wrapped, before anybody knew how big a hit *Baby Jane* would be, Bette hoped the good word-of-mouth about the film would help jump-start her career. Taking no chances, she immediately placed a tongue-in-cheek ad in movie trade publications:

> MOTHER OF THREE - 10, 11 & 15 - DIVORCEE. AMERICAN. THIRTY YEARS EXPERIENCE AS AN ACTRESS IN MOTION PICTURES. MOBILE STILL AND MORE AFFABLE THAN RUMOR WOULD HAVE IT. WANTS STEADY EMPLOYMENT IN HOLLYWOOD. (HAS HAD BROADWAY.) Bette Davis, c/o Martin Baum, G.A.C. REFERENCES UPON REQUEST.

The industry laughed on cue, but there was a note of seriousness in the advertisement. She wanted to make sure that producers and directors thought of her as they cast prestigious films, rather than simply tossing her the dregs. But her satirical humor was misunderstood. Many people thought it was only accidentally funny, as if she didn't know she was making a fool of herself.

Though *Baby Jane* did boost her career, not all the movies Bette was offered were gems – but eager to be working, she accepted. In 1963's *The Empty Canvas,* a sex-focused Italian film, she played a small role as the domineering mother of the male lead ("Empty it was," Bette said later). The following year, Bette appeared in an American drama, *Where Love Has Gone*, playing a selfish, conniving mother whose meddling ruins her daughter's marriage and life.

What the success of *Baby Jane* did, more than anything, was make filmmakers think of her for creepy stories. In 1964's *Dead Ringer*, directed by her *Now, Voyager* co-star Paul Henreid, Bette played a set of twins, just as she had nearly two decades earlier in *A Stolen Life*. This time, one of the twins kills and impersonates the other.

Even scarier was another 1964 film with the working title *What Ever Happened to Cousin Charlotte?*, the latest in what would become known as the "Psycho-biddy" genre that officially began with *Baby Jane* – movies that feature a once-glamorous older woman who goes crazy and terrorizes everybody around her (the genre was also known as "hagsploitation" or "hag horror").

*Cousin Charlotte* was co-written by Henry Farrell, author of the novel that *Baby Jane* was based upon. Farrell had written an unpublished short story about an aging recluse named Charlotte Hollis who suffers from terrible memories and hallucinations. Living in the house where her married lover was beheaded and mutilated by an unknown assailant, she seeks help from her cousin Miriam - who plots to drive Charlotte mad so she can inherit her property.

*Baby Jane* director Robert Aldrich thought this would be the perfect follow-up, and hoped both Bette and Crawford would agree to a reunion. But the roles would be reversed this time, with Crawford playing the devious, manipulative relative and Bette the victim.

When Aldrich approached Bette, she flatly refused, saying she would never work with Crawford again - and, besides, she added, Crawford was wrong for the part. She also hated the title. *What Ever Happened to Cousin Charlotte?* was such an obvious reference to the earlier film that it smacked of opportunism and lack of creativity.

But later, Bette called Aldrich to say she changed her mind. "Robert, I will accept Crawford, if you will change the title to *Hush . . . Hush, Sweet Charlotte,*" she said, appropriating the name of a love song featured in the film. She also wanted a production credit. Aldrich at first refused, then finally agreed.

Crawford, who needed the money, agreed to participate, too. But she soon became convinced that Bette was trying to extract revenge for her humiliation at the 1963 Oscars. She believed Bette was sleeping with Aldrich to get him on her side and conspiring with the crew to deny Crawford the star treatment she was famous for demanding in every film. How else to explain why nobody picked her up from the Baton Rouge airport when she arrived for a location shoot?

As it turns out, Bette *was*, indeed, scheming to turn the cast and crew against her. For instance, on the last day of shooting, Crawford went back to her trailer and took a nap. When she woke up, she was alone. Everyone else had wrapped up and headed back to the hotel – a cruel joke, courtesy of Bette.

When she got back to Los Angeles, Crawford checked into a hospital, upset that Bette was doing the same thing Crawford's character was doing to Charlotte in the movie – trying to drive her mad. Crawford had also been demanding changes to the script, so her absence was interpreted as a strike until concessions were made. According to the gossip columnists, she had her clothes made daily and her food catered by The Brown Derby. The doctors could find nothing wrong with her, but at some point, Crawford managed to convince herself she really *was* sick.

With production of *Sweet Charlotte* suspended during Crawford's hospitalization, Aldrich hired a private investigator to find out if her illness was real. When the gumshoe concluded she was faking, Aldrich decided to fire her. It was either that or shut down production – and the director was determined to move forward.

At first, Aldrich wanted Vivien Leigh, but Bette objected, saying she would be just as temperamental as Crawford. She was far more approving of his next choice, her good friend Olivia de Havilland.

So Aldrich spent four days at de Havilland's home in Switzerland and, after much hesitation, the actress finally agreed.

When Crawford learned she had been let go – on the radio, no less – she told the press that she cried for hours. She complained about what a harsh industry it was, and vowed that, from then on, she would only make movies with kinder people.

After a three-month delay, production of *Sweet Charlotte* resumed. Shooting was much smoother now, as Bette and de Havilland got along well. But the role was challenging for Bette. Though her character did not commit the grisly murder at the heart of the story, she has to make the audience believe she might have, even though she had no obvious motive. "I tell you, it was one of the most difficult parts I have ever played," Bette declared to the British Film Institute's *Sight and Sound* magazine.

The film opened in December of 1964 to glowing reviews. *Variety* praised Bette's "outstanding performance" while the critic Kenneth Tynan said she "has done nothing better since *The Little Foxes*" more than two decades earlier. The film wasn't as profitable as *Baby Jane* but still did well at the box office: $4 million in revenue on a budget of $2.2 million. It was also nominated for seven Academy Awards (though none for Bette).

While the professional drama of shooting *Sweet Charlotte* was happening, a personal drama was unfolding in Bette's family life: Her eldest child, B.D., fell madly in love with an older man Bette strenuously objected to.

The romance started in May of 1963, while Bette was promoting *Baby Jane*. She brought her daughter, who had just turned sixteen, to the Cannes Film Festival, where the film would be presented. B.D. was excited to be making the trip with her mother, having had a bit part in the film playing a neighbor girl.

Since B.D. needed an escort to the showing of the film, the producer of *Sweet Charlotte*, Eliot Hyman, sent his twenty-nine-year-old nephew, Jeremy Hyman, who worked for him at Seven Arts Productions. Jeremy, in no mood to be a baby-sitter, was unhappy about the assignment. But when Bette opened the door of her suite at the Carlton hotel, he was dazzled by the sight of an attractive young woman who did not need baby-sitting at all. B.D. was immediately smitten by the handsome Brit who said, "I am Jeremy Hyman. I have come to escort Miss Sherry to the showing tonight."

As they stared at each other, "something was happening," Bette said later, "but in the rush and excitement of leaving for the theater, I forgot about it." After the festival, Bette and B.D. went to Paris for a week. Jeremy joined them soon after they arrived, and the love-struck couple barely let their feet touch the ground as they floated through the most romantic city in the world. Though B.D. was thirteen years his junior, Jeremy was entranced by his new girlfriend's intelligence, poise, charm, and youthful sensuality.

When Jeremy returned to his home in London, B.D. was able to meet him there, since Bette had business in the city. By now, they were already talking about getting married, which shocked Bette – she was heartbroken that her daughter would consider marrying and moving away at such a tender young age. "I took it for granted she would be with me at least until she was twenty-one," she said later.

Bette also didn't like the way Jeremy ordered B.D. around and was stunned that her normally assertive daughter meekly accepted it. One morning in Paris, when B.D. and Jeremy were having breakfast on the terrace of the hotel room, Bette noticed that Jeremy was doing all the talking. But Bette knew there was nothing she could do to stop a marriage.

Mother and daughter finally flew back to California, but a few months later, when Bette went to Italy to make the film *The Empty Canvas*, B.D. came with her, and they stopped off in London on the way. There, they met Jeremy and his mother, who heartily approved of B.D., and the couple fell even more deeply in love. When they arrived in Italy - and B.D. came down with appendicitis - she insisted on returning to London for the operation. By the time they flew back to California, Jeremy had formally proposed marriage and B.D. had accepted.

By now, Bette had come to accept the union as inevitable and threw an engagement party for the couple at the ritzy Hotel Bel-Air. Since B.D. was underage, Bette had to sign documents giving her permission to marry. "This I did with great reluctance," she recalled, "but I felt (that) if the marriage failed she would, I hoped, have had a rewarding experience."

B.D. and Jeremy were married in January of 1964 at an Episcopal church in Beverly Hills.

It was an extravagant affair. B.D. wore a sleeveless wedding dress from the luxury retailer I. Magnin & Co., which featured a veil of handmade lace from Marseilles. Five of B.D.'s cousins were bridesmaids, her eleven-year-old brother Michael was the ring bearer - and Bobby's daughter Faye was the maid of honor. Jeremy's family flew in from New York and London. Estranged from both her father (William Sherry) and stepfather (Gary Merrill), B.D. chose to walk down the aisle alone.

At the reception at the Beverly Wilshire Hotel, the bride and groom were toasted with Dom Perignon. They spent their wedding night at the Beverly Hills Hotel, where Bette decided to play practical jokes. She put iced tea in the scotch bottle, clear tape on all the water spouts, and black satin sheets on the bed since Jeremy had once said he thought they were sexy.

But when Bette returned home that night, she was devastated, feeling that she had lost her daughter. Unable to sleep, she spent the night on her chaise in the living room, chain-smoking and staring into space. She thought about how much she loved having her daughter around the house, remembered their fun times together, and how B.D. would come home after a date so eager to tell her all about it. "I have never up to then, or since, felt so alone," she said.

Later, Bette wrote the lyrics to a song about how she felt during the ceremony. "Mother of the Bride" was included in *Miss Bette Davis*, an album of music she recorded in England and released in the United Sates many years later, in 1983. (Bette was not much of a singer, so many of the tunes were spoken more than sung.) The self-pitying lyrics read, in part:

> *She's been the comfort of my life*
>
> *What shall I do without her?*
>
> *Oh, she looks so beautiful and so young*
>
> *Why must she leave me so soon?*
>
> *Haven't I always been a good mother to her?*

*Haven't I done everything in the world for her?*

*Did I do all those things, spend all those years, only to lose her?*

There was more sadness for Bette. Six months after the wedding, she visited B.D. in New York, where she had moved with Jeremy. The phone rang, and her daughter began talking to someone she called "Daddy." When she hung up, B.D. explained that her father, William Sherry, was visiting New York and would be coming by that afternoon.

Bette was shocked. Her daughter had not mentioned that they were in touch, and neither of them had seen Sherry since B.D. was three years old. Bette asked her daughter if she could stay to see him and B.D. agreed. "I simply had to see what he looked like," Bette said later."

When he arrived, it was an awkward scene, but Sherry gave his daughter hugs and kisses. Then he asked to speak to Bette alone. They went into another room.

"I must apologize for how horribly I treated you years ago," Sherry said. Bette wasn't sure what to say. "It's water under the bridge," she blurted out. "Just forget it."

Back in the living room, Bette and Sherry sat on the couch and B.D. sat on the arm. Looking at them, she said, "I never thought in my life I would ever again be in the same room with my own father and mother."

Bette excused herself and went back to her room at the Plaza Hotel. It was an innocent remark, Bette knew, but it still hurt her deeply. She cried uncontrollably, remembering how badly B.D.'s father had treated her and realizing that those childhood years were now gone forever, the damage beyond fixing.

B.D.'s new bond with her father would not last. Sherry had become a Jehovah's Witness and began sending her streams of pamphlets and other proselytizing materials. Put off by his conversion attempts, B.D. let the relationship fizzle out once more.

B.D. was growing more distant from her mother, too, as she tried to prove that she was a big, independent girl. In fact, she was egged on by Jeremy who could clearly see that his mother-in-law was having trouble letting go; he wanted to create some space.

With B.D gone, Bette would have preferred to stay busy with work. But her big-screen comeback that began with *Baby Jane* and continued with *Sweet Charlotte* had stalled again. Old Hollywood had faded away - and television had transformed the entertainment landscape.

There was little demand for an actress entering her sixties. Over the next decade, between 1965 and 1975, Bette would make only five films - *The Nanny*, *The Anniversary*, *Connecting Rooms*, *Bunny O'Hare*, and *The Scientific Cardplayer* - and her career was becoming more notable for the roles she did *not* get than the ones she did.

Bette had been considered for the 1957 Broadway production of *Look Homeward, Angel* - the same show she had planned to do in Los Angeles before her fall down the stairs - but Jo Van Fleet, seven years younger, was chosen. Bette also was suggested for a screen adaptation of Tennessee Williams's *Suddenly Last Summer*, released in 1959, but it went to Katharine Hepburn. Bette declined John Huston's offer to play Mrs. Zachary in 1960's *The Unforgiven* because she couldn't bring herself to play Burt Lancaster's mother. (Lillian Gish, fifteen years older than Bette, took the part.)

Bette also was a strong contender for the iconic role of Martha in the 1966 film version of Edward Albee's classic play, *Who's Afraid of Virginia Woolf?*, which ultimately went to Elizabeth Taylor. Albee recalled Jack Warner telling him that he was buying the rights to the play with Bette and James Mason in mind for the leads - but later, he decided that Taylor and Richard Burton had more star power. (Albee's one regret was that he never got to see Bette mimicking herself in the film's opening beats, when Martha bellows, "What a dump!")

Astonishingly, another film for which Bette was

considered was 1964's *Mary Poppins*. She was Walt Disney's choice for the legendary Julie Andrews role, though today it's hard to imagine the churlish Bette singing sweetly to birds outside the window as she gently urges the children to clean their room.

In many ways, it was the film industry's loss that she didn't work more during this time. There was no other actress like her – someone who could portray women with such powerful undercurrents lurking beneath the surface, just waiting to erupt. Her cigarette smoking, fidgeting, voice fluctuation, and expressive eyes created a style that was mesmerizing, almost hypnotic at times. But with her upright posture and ability to simply freeze over and glare, she was also capable of remarkable restraint.

But her reputation as a hellion on the set caught up with her, as fewer producers were willing to risk an expensive film production on such an explosive personality. Though she was never clinically diagnosed, some have suggested that Bette may have had some form of borderline personality disorder, which distorts a person's view of oneself and others and can quickly destroy relationships.

Bette, it seemed, could often not tell the difference between which of her fears were legitimate and which were baseless paranoia. Beyond her frequent tantrums, she had trouble dealing with authority and seemed to be on a mission to make life as miserable for others as it was for her. Bette's troubled and suspicious relationships with men - not just husbands but directors and co-stars - may have been rooted in her father's abandonment and her turbulent childhood. Her excessive drinking only made it worse.

All these factors intruded on even her deepest relationships, including the one with her sister Bobby. As the years passed, feelings between them became strained and Bette treated her coldly. Chuck Pollack, a designer-decorator who became a close friend of Bette's in the late sixties and early seventies, said that she was often angry and didn't trust anyone, not even Bobby. It was surprising to see Bette treat her sister so horribly, Pollack said, because Bobby had often helped care for her children in times of need.

Bobby moved to Phoenix in 1971, and the sisters eventually stopped communicating. Before Bobby died of cancer in 1979, Bette was informed that her sister was gravely ill but chose not to visit her before her death.

Bette's relationship with her daughter Margo, meanwhile, was also problematic, as her patience in dealing with a severely disabled child was very short. Margot could do crafts and write letters but was far from being able to relate to her mother as an adult. Bette had to constantly remind herself to use a gentler voice and shorter sentences when talking to her daughter. It was hard for both of them. Margot often came home earlier than expected from her visits with Bette, said Mary Beardsley, a housemother at Lochland. Sometimes the girl even arrived with a vocabulary of new swear words – and a certain sadness about the way her mom had treated her.

Bette and Merrill had planned to bring Margot home by the time she aged out of the Lochland School. But by 1969, when Margot turned eighteen, they were long divorced and Lochland had started a program for adults. Merrill wanted to keep her there, but Bette preferred she stay at a facility called Devereaux California in Santa Barbara.

In the ensuing fight, Bette refused to pay for her care if Merrill insisted on Lochland. He prevailed and paid the bills. Later, Merrill accused Bette of abandoning their child, though in her memoir *This 'N That*, she said Margot came home often, "and our times together have been happy."

One relationship that did improve for a while – before it got much, much worse – was with B.D and Jeremy. A few years after their wedding, the couple moved from New York to Weston, Connecticut. Soon afterward, B.D. asked her mom if she would agree to let her look for a house for her in the area. "I was thrilled," Bette remembered. "Obviously, the 'quarantine' was over." But to keep things that way, she knew she would have to behave herself and avoid being an intrusive mother-in-law.

So B.D. shopped around and found her a new home. When Bette arrived, B.D. picked her up at the airport and drove her directly to her new place. Bette loved it. The house was near a river and was the perfect size for her and Michael, who would stay there during vacations from college at the University of North Carolina at Chapel Hill. "It was sensational feeling like a mother again," Bette said.

More happy news arrived with the birth of B.D.'s first child, in June of 1969. Bette doted on the boy, named J. Ashley Hyman. When Ashley turned two, Bette was allowed to spend one day a week with him, taking him to the edge of the river to make mud pies. For a while, family bliss reigned. Bette and B.D. would go shopping together, make wreaths at Christmas, and spend happy days at what Bette called B.D.'s "warm, inviting home, loved by all who visited her."

It would not last. A few years later, the Hymans decided they wanted a more rural lifestyle, so they bought a farm in Laceyville, Pennsylvania, in the Endless Mountains. Only half-joking, Bette asked her daughter and son-in-law, "To what lengths are you going to eliminate me as a neighbor?"

The line was funny at the time, but Bette's relationship with her daughter would eventually rupture so badly that it became no laughing matter. The same was true of most of Bette's closest relationships. It's no wonder that she called her first autobiography *The Lonely Life*. She certainly felt that way when the book was published in 1962, but as the years went on, her life would get even lonelier.

# 17

# "OLD AGE AIN'T NO PLACE FOR SISSIES."

As Bette entered her sixth and seventh decades, her obstinate behavior left her increasingly isolated. But the very qualities that repelled those close to her - a brutal frankness and insistence that things be done *her* way - made her an object of fascination, even admiration, to fans and others beyond her immediate circle. It was during these years, as Bette became more entrenched in her anti-social ways, that she enjoyed some of her greatest fame.

Bette's romantic life, never smooth, took on an air of farce as she aged, becoming odder and odder.

Case in point: As she approached age sixty, with four attempts at marriage behind her, she had few illusions about love. But Bette also had trouble resisting marriage proposals that came her away.

For example, one such proposal came from a younger Catholic man whose possessive mother objected to the fact that Bette was not Catholic (not to mention their wide age difference). So Bette converted to Catholicism. She met with a priest in her suite at the Plaza Hotel in New York, ready to have a sober discussion about how to lead the righteous life of a Catholic. But the priest was so excited at being in the same room with the famous Bette Davis that he consumed far too much scotch. As she helped the Father weave out the door, Bette realized that her religious conversion – and the love affair that inspired it – were not going to work out.

The second proposal came from a man who accompanied her to England, where Bette was making a movie. One night, as they sipped cocktails together, Bette remembered a promise she had made to her lawyer: She would not marry again without a prenuptial agreement. So she breathed deeply and said, "There are papers you have to sign before our marriage."

"What do you mean?" the man said.

"You must sign a premarital agreement," Bette replied. "These papers will confirm what's mine is mine and so forth."

The next day, she went off to work. When she returned to the hotel that evening, the clerk said her fiancé had checked out. "It was a terrible blow to my pride," she said later. "That was the last time I have given marriage any serious thought."

Bette had other affairs, of course, but her growing penchant for younger men led to some humiliating situations. One New Year's holiday, she rented a house at Lake Arrowhead in Southern California and invited her young lover and a group of friends. When they went antiquing together, Bette bought a bureau for her home. The shopkeeper, excited that the famous movie star was in her store, said, "Would you and your son care for a drink?"

There were, of course, other humiliations.

By now, Bette had become an icon among gay movie fans, possibly because many of her movies, like *Baby Jane*, were so campy. This created new awkward moments in her love life: Handsome men would, for instance, shower attention on Bette. For some reason, she did not realize they were gay. So Bette told Robin Brown, a close friend since their teen summers in Maine, to let her know whenever such uncomfortable situations arose. She did, but that rarely stopped Bette, who would insist that she could change the man's orientation. Bette even once proposed to her good friend Chuck Pollack, a gay designer-decorator in Los Angeles, who said later that she seemed to only half-understand the notion that people could be attracted to members of their own sex.

With her marrying days over, Bette came to rely heavily on her friends.

Yet she could be extremely trying, even to those closest to her. Her most loyal friends found ways to tolerate her mercurial, abrasive ways, but when she drank, that was not easy. Her longtime personal assistant, Vik Greenfield, said that when Bette was in a bad mood, she took it out on everyone within thrashing distance. Greenfield added that he wasn't sure how she had any friends left at all.

Robin Brown was Bette's longest-lasting friend. She was a kind, subdued, and smart woman who stood at five feet two inches and could look straight into Bette's eyes. Bette didn't always treat her like the treasure that she was, Greenfield said, adding that Brown's husband always dreaded when they had to go out to dinner with Bette.

The actress Ellen Hanley, who became close to Bette when she moved to Connecticut, noticed that Bette could do a Jekyll-and-Hyde act when she started drinking at lunchtime. She liked screwdrivers with her lunch and was sure to undergo an immediate personality change soon thereafter. Hanley said aging was frustrating for Bette and she seemed to have a lot of anxiety.

One source of joy for Bette was her son Michael,

who began coming home from college at UNC Chapel Hill more often, making the 600-mile drive to Westport, Connecticut on weekends. But it wasn't his mom he was eager to see. It was a woman who lived on the same street named Charlene Raum, whom everybody called Chou Chou.

As Michael's graduation approached in the spring of 1973, he made two big decisions – to marry Chou Chou and to attend law school at Boston University in the fall. Bette implored him to finish law school first, before marriage, but he was unswayed. Michael knew full well that his mother had given his older sister B.D. permission to wed at sixteen.

Michael and Chou Chou were married in May of that year at the Westport Congregational Church in front of two dozen of his fraternity brothers who drove all the way from Chapel Hill. His father Gary Merrill was also there and stood with Bette at the head of the reception line.

Bette thought Merrill looked much better than he did four years earlier, at Michael's graduation from a prep school in Windsor, Connecticut. On that day, he had shown up unshaven, wearing a watermelon-colored jacket, brightly printed yellow tie, gold shoes, and carrying a red squirt gun to promote his latest film project, called *Cycad*, which never made it to the screen.

Now, at Michael's wedding, Bette noticed that her ex-husband seemed to have "regained control of his life and was once more the attractive man I had met during the filming of *All About Eve*."

With Michael off at law school, Bette's house was quiet and lonely again. Around that time, she called her actress friend Hanley asking for help with a dramatic situation that was about to make Bette even sadder. She had received a box of letters that Ruthie had written to a friend and wanted Hanley to be there when she read them. The box had been found in an attic in Maine, and the new homeowners thought Bette might want them.

Bette dreaded what she'd find in the letters, but she read them anyway. That may have been a mistake. Some of the letters cut her deeply. They spoke of Bette as a burden and a joke, some of them very sarcastic. Bette didn't even know the recipient of the letters, which made them all the more painful. When she was finished, Bette was heartbroken and fuming. Having polished off a screwdriver, she began screaming that she couldn't believe her mother would say such things after all she'd done for her.

With Michael no longer coming home to Westport on weekends, Bette began spending more time in Los Angeles, staying with her good friend Pollack. But that didn't seem to make her any happier. Bette was best early in the day, Pollack recalled, before she'd had too many drinks – though she usually had vodka in her orange juice in the mornings. By lunchtime, he said, she was usually drinking straight vodka, which would last until cocktail hour, when she'd switch to scotch. She was far more pleasant when she was staying sober for work purposes. If she was to appear on a talk show, for example, she would avoid drinking for the day and could handle it perfectly.

Though liquor may have temporarily made Bette feel better, it made her behavior worse. Pollack remembered a time when she wanted to help him in the garden but ended up chopping up plants and killing them, like her deranged character in *Baby Jane*. Or if someone had sent flowers to the house, she'd get fidgety and pick off all the blooms until none were left. She would beg him to invite people over and then do nothing but insult them until telling them all to go home. Pollack remembered the shock on the faces of the guests as they left.

With her personal life miserable, Bette tried to find solace in professional accomplishment. But Los Angeles in the 1970s was a different place than the one Bette knew during the Golden Age of Hollywood in the thirties and forties. There was little work for her in feature films, so she increasingly turned to television. She was offered numerous Movie of the Week scripts that she insisted were at least as good as those for the big screen. But she may have been trying to convince herself, afraid of becoming one of those old-timers rhapsodizing about the good old days. "No matter how we romanticize them, the golden years were hard work, as they are today," she insisted later. "The fight is still between the artists and the money men."

But Bette couldn't keep from feeling a bit nostalgic for the old studio system – which is ironic given that she had fought so hard against it. Though she felt abused by the studios, she had to admit they helped her develop her craft by forcing her to crank out one film after another. And the elaborate publicity machinery managed to make an unknown actress from Lowell, Massachusetts into an international star.

As television came of age, Bette appeared on many of the major shows – *General Electric Theater, Alfred Hitchcock Presents, Perry Mason, Gunsmoke, The Virginian*, and *Wagon Train*. The one episode of *Gunsmoke* she appeared in, "The Jailer" – as a belligerent old woman avenging her husband's death – was ranked by *TV Guide* as one of the "100 Greatest (Television) Episodes of All Time."

Conditions on the set could be grueling, especially compared to the pampered treatment she received at the Warner Brothers lot back in the old days. While shooting TV Westerns, she didn't even get a dressing room. Actors had to wait for hours between shots out in the open, with dust, grime, and horse droppings. "You not only acted like a pioneer woman, you felt like one," she said later.

Bette's TV roles served a dual function: They paid the bills and kept her in the public eye, where she continued to play a role she had spent her whole life developing: herself. By now, the hard-drinking, chain-smoking, blunt-talking, grand dame of Hollywood had become perhaps the most compelling character she had ever created. All the talk-show hosts wanted her – Johnny Carson, Mike Douglas, Merv Griffin, Dick Cavett – and she also appeared on *Laugh-In* and variety shows hosted by show-biz legends such as Jimmy Durante and Milton Berle.

Being Bette Davis turned out to be such a big audience draw that she decided to capitalize on it, creating an international theatrical tour that lasted, on and off, for five years. The concept began in February of 1973 when a film publicist named John Springer decided to host a series of events in New York City featuring Hollywood stars called *Legendary Ladies of the Movies*. Each evening, a different star – Myrna Loy, Rosalind Russell, Lana Turner, Joan Crawford, Sylvia Sidney, and Bette – got up on stage to discuss her career and answer questions from the audience. When it was Bette's turn, the show was a smash hit. At one point, a group of gay men rushed to the stage, shouting her name, holding Bette dolls and *Baby Jane* dolls. Some even dressed up like Bette.

The success of that night inspired Springer and Bette to take the show on the road. They booked it in twenty-six states in the U.S. and spent six months in England and two weeks in Australia. Wherever she went, Bette made people laugh. "I cannot explain why so many come whenever or wherever I appear," she said later. "But then, I could not explain a career that has lasted over fifty years."

In Perth, Australia, a woman asked, "Miss Davis, why do people have such strong emotions about you? My husband wouldn't come with me tonight because he hates you." Bette was unfazed. "My dear, one can never be a success in my profession if everyone likes you," she replied. "When you get home tell your husband he is one of many who feel the same way about me."

In the late 1970s, as she approached seventy, Bette became increasingly celebrated for her remarkable career and singular personality. She became the first woman to receive the Lifetime Achievement Award from the American Film Institute. That televised 1977 event included tributes from Jane Fonda, Henry Fonda, Natalie Wood, Olivia de Havilland, and William Wyler. Even President Ronald Reagan, who knew Bette when they were both contract players at Warner Brothers, sent his congratulations via videotape. "I must say, even though I am a Democrat," Bette said later, "the president's speech touched me very much."

That high-profile event led to an impressive late-career resurgence for Bette, starting with a two-part television miniseries, *The Dark Secret of Harvest Home*, and the Agatha Cristie murder mystery *Death on the Nile*, both released in 1978. The latter was an old-fashioned, big-screen feature with an all-star cast that included Peter Ustinov, Mia Farrow, Maggie Smith, Angela Lansbury, David Niven, and George Kennedy – and Bette was so thrilled she could barely sleep the night before production began.

Filmed on location in Egypt, *Death on the Nile* took seven weeks to shoot. Work began early each day with a makeup call at 4:00 a.m., to avoid the searing mid-day desert heat that reached 115 degrees Fahrenheit. Never a big fan of filming in exotic locales, Bette missed the comforts of the studio. "In the older days, they'd have built the Nile for you," she grumbled. Though *Death on the Nile* did not match the huge success of another Agatha Christie film, 1974's *Murder on the Orient Express*, it did reasonably well and won an Academy Award for costume design.

Soon after that, Bette made a rare appearance in a children's film - Disney's *Return from Witch Mountain*, about kids with supernatural powers. Then she won her first and only Emmy award for

1979's TV drama *Strangers: The Story of a Mother and Daughter,* about a bitter New England widow who reunites with her daughter who has cancer.

During that busy period of making films, Bette turned seventy - and her behavior became even more eccentric. She decided to throw a party with a black theme that reflected her mood: She placed a black wreath on the front door, wore a black dress, blackened her face with makeup, and donned a black Afro wig. "Being seventy made me feel as if I should be in mourning," she explained.

But Bette was not the type to give up on her career merely because she was getting older. "Age, I believe I can truthfully say, has not done much to bank whatever fires burned inside me," she wrote in *This 'N That*.

Bette's place as a cultural icon was further cemented in 1981 when Kim Carnes had a smash hit with the song, *Bette Davis Eyes*. Co-written years earlier by Donna Weiss and Jackie DeShannon, the tune was inspired by the famous cigarette-lighting scene in *Now, Voyager*. DeShannon had made her own recording of the song in 1974, but it was not a hit until Carnes released her version, which hit number one in the United States and stayed there for two months.

As *Bette Davis Eyes* began getting airplay, people kept asking Bette herself if she had heard it. When she finally listened, she was struck by the lyrics, "She'll expose you when she snows you/Off your feet with the crumbs that she throws you." So she wrote a note to the composers saying, "How did you know so much about me?" When Carnes won a gold record, then a platinum one, she graciously sent a framed copy of each to Bette, who hung them on the wall of her trophy room.

Despite her age, Bette was getting what she had always craved: sustained attention. That she usually got it at the expense of her personal life had always been a traumatic trade-off, but she did what she could to maintain a sense of family. In 1982, she rented a house on Long Island for the summer and invited her children B.D. and Michael to visit with their families on the Fourth of July weekend. By now, B.D.'s son Ashley was thirteen years old and her second child, Justin, was nearly five. Michael came with Chou Chou and their one-year-old baby, Matthew (another son, Cameron, would be born two years later). It was the first time the families had all been together in years.

For four days, Bette was delighted. She cooked, and the kids played croquet and tennis, swam in the bay, collected mussels, and rode the swings she had installed on the property. She served lobsters, and they all watched the spectacular fireworks, courtesy of the town of Huntington. "It was four days I will always treasure," she said later. Once they had all left, however, Bette plunged back into loneliness and sadness again.

The sense that life is precious and fleeting was even more apparent to Bette the next year, as she was preparing to accept yet another accolade, the Charles Chaplin Award for Lifetime Achievement. That's when she found a lump in one of her breasts. X-rays later confirmed that she had cancer.

"To say I was in a state of shock is putting it mildly," she said later. At age seventy-five, Bette was beginning one of the most torturous chapters in her life. Now she understood, more deeply than ever, the truth of the quip she is most famous for: "Old age ain't no place for sissies."

# 18
# "MISS DAVIS, WE ALL LOVE YOU."

As she struggled to cope with the devastating news of her cancer diagnosis, Bette was determined to fulfill her commitments to appear at various award ceremonies scheduled in her honor during the spring of 1983. Though she did not tell many people about her condition, it seemed as if, with each accolade bestowed upon her, Hollywood was saying goodbye.

She decided to undergo surgery in New York. When it was time to leave for the airport, she lingered in her doorway, wondering if she would ever return home.

On June 9, Bette had a mastectomy at New York Hospital. As she recovered, she thanked God that she had discovered the lump early, before the cancer had spread, and that the surgery was successful. For now, the disease was gone.

“I had been lucky in my life,” she mused. “Now I was lucky again.”

But her luck soon ran out. Nine days after the surgery, Bette suffered a stroke. Her condition was serious; the doctors were not sure if she would pull through. She survived but was now severely disabled. As she lay in bed, she thought of her last film, a made-for-TV movie called *Right of Way,* with Jimmy Stewart. They played a long-married couple who make a suicide pact after Bette's character is diagnosed with a terminal illness. “It happens that I am tired,” Stewart's character says. “I am tired of my feet and my nails and my hair and my shadow. It happens that I am tired of being a man. I'm tired of living.”

That's how Bette felt after the stroke. She figured that, at age seventy-five, she was nearing the end of her life anyway. “What was the point of the long struggle ahead?” she thought. “To learn to walk again? To unknot my left hand so I could use it again?” It all seemed pointless.

Later, one of Bette's friends broke down weeping as he told her, “The first time I saw you after the stroke, Bette Davis wasn't in that bed. She was gone.”

In her hospital room, one sleepless night after

another, she wondered, "Why me?" Would she become a burden to her children and friends? But one question haunted her more than any other: "Will I ever work again?" To Bette, acting was everything. "I wouldn't want to live if I could never act again," she realized.

During her long, slow recovery,ww Bette had lots of time to think, especially about the many characters she had played. She thought about *Dark Victory*'s Judith Traherne, who faced death so bravely. Bette wanted to be like her. She also thought about the mistakes she had made in her personal life, such as marrying William Sherry and Gary Merrill, who had both treated Bette and her daughter B.D. terribly. That must be why B.D. married an older man, Bette finally admitted: She was looking for the father she never had.

But Bette didn't give up – thanks to Kathryn Sermak. Bette had hired the young woman as her assistant four years earlier, soon after her graduation from the University of Southern California. Now twenty-six, Sermak gave Bette pep talks every day, almost every hour: "We'll make it!" she would cry.

As Bette said later, "Kathryn literally saved my life."

Cheered on by Kathryn, Bette began getting better. When she began shouting at the nurses and doctors – angry over their intrusive visits to her room, the drugs that made her woozy, the way they bossed her around – the worried staff discussed giving her a sedative. But Kathryn just smiled; Bette's tantrums were a sure sign she was improving.

After nine long weeks in the hospital, Bette was finally released. She left in a wheelchair, eight pounds lighter than when she checked in, and was driven straight to her temporary new home, the Lombardy Hotel in midtown. As her car wound its way through the streets of Manhattan, Bette wept with joy at the sight of trees preparing to turn their fall colors, people strolling on the streets, the fresh air wafting through her window. When they arrived at the hotel, she was thrilled to be in a suite of comfortably furnished rooms with room service and no nosy doctors bothering her. It even had a terrace where she could sit and soak up the sun.

Recovering from her stroke, however, was a grueling process. She could not tie her shoes or button a blouse without Kathryn's help, which made her feel like a child. It took her three months to regain use of her left hand. When she could finally use a fork and knife, she celebrated. With daily therapy, she learned to walk again. And for a full month, she did not drink or smoke, a feat few thought possible.

Before her surgery, Bette had finished filming the pilot for a television drama, *Hotel*. As the weekly series went on without her character, hotel owner Laura Trent, her fans wrote asking when she would return. Bette thought the show was awful but desperately wanted to go back to work and told producer Aaron Spelling she would return in January. Eventually, however, discouraged by the quality of scripts, Bette informed him that she would not be back, after all. (The show ranked in Nielsen's top twenty-five programs for the first three seasons, but fell to ninety-first by season five and was promptly canceled.)

Bette continued to improve thanks to her usual stalwart supporters, her son Michael and Kathryn. Just before Thanksgiving, she was ready to fly back to Los Angeles. When she arrived and opened the door to her home, she was overcome with happiness at being back in familiar surroundings. After a five-month absence, she now cherished her favorite possessions, like the photos on the walls of her posing with Mae West, Beverly Sills, and the late Egyptian President Anwar Sadat.

Her joy was short-lived, however. One day, she fell and broke her hip. Bette was rushed to the hospital for another operation. When she returned home a few days later, she could not walk. Bette was crushed. After all those months of hard work to recover from her stroke, she was an invalid again.

The accident happened just as Kathryn was leaving for a vacation with her boyfriend. Bette missed her terribly, even though she had help from a nurse, various cooks she could not manage to keep for very long, and her hairdresser and friend Peggy Shannon. She refused all requests for visits from other friends – she did not want them to see her in such a weakened condition. She did not eat well and lost weight. "All my film career I had envied Katharine Hepburn's high cheekbones and narrow face," she quipped. "Now I had them."

Things got worse when Kathryn moved to San Francisco. Though she flew back often to visit on weekends, Bette had trouble surviving without her. She could not find a replacement as kind, understanding, and competent – and able to put up with her mood swings and demands. Many simply stopped showing up to work soon after being hired.

Fortunately, Kathryn moved back to Los Angeles and decided that what Bette really needed was a house on the beach. They found a lovely place for Bette in Malibu, surrounded by cacti, palm trees, banana trees, and geraniums. "Living by the ocean again, where I had lived so often in former years, and which I adored, turned out to be exactly what I needed for my complete recovery," Bette said later.

It was mid-July of 1984, just over a year after her surgery, when Bette moved into her new home. Inspired by the beautiful natural surroundings, she began entertaining again. One night, she held a dinner party and invited some of her old celebrity friends, including Robert Wagner, Roddy

McDowall, and Jill St. John. Before the party, she was nervous about how she would look to them after all she had been through. She needn't have worried. Everyone had a great time, and her friends said she looked like the old Bette they knew and loved. Life seemed back to normal.

Another good sign occurred the day she and Kathryn went shopping and stopped at a restaurant for lunch. Spotting her, some fans swarmed around Bette, asking for her autograph. "I can't believe it," she told Kathryn later. "I have missed being famous and made a fuss over!"

Perhaps the biggest turning point came when Bette decided to go swimming. Kathryn had found an apartment near Bette's house – so she could help out as often as possible – and there was a pool on the premises. Bette was terrified as she gingerly eased into the water, but knew she must do it. Despite her new hip and a weak left arm, she found that she could actually swim. Tears welled up in Kathryn's eyes. When Bette climbed out, they exchanged wet hugs and kisses. "Miss D., we made it!" Kathryn cried.

For Bette, the final hurdle to resuming a normal life was getting back to work. A few months earlier, on New Year's Eve she and Kathryn had taken part in a Davis family ritual of writing down a wish and then, at midnight, throwing the paper into the fireplace. Bette's wish was that she would make a film in the New Year of 1984 – and hoped it would be made in England. As the months passed, nothing happened. Her career, it seemed, was over.

Then, in late September, a script arrived at her Malibu home. It was for another Agatha Christie story, *Murder with Mirrors*. She loved the script, adored her part, and was thrilled with the idea of working with the eighty-four -year-old legend Helen Hayes (in what would be Hayes's final film role).

By then, it had been nearly two years since Bette's last acting job, in *Hotel*, one of the longest dry spells of her career. She was alternately excited and terrified. "Could I make the long days on the set?" she wondered. "Could I remember the lines?"

Filming would start in less than three weeks – in England, of all places, just as she had wished. That seemed like a good omen. When she sat down with the script, she found she was able to memorize the whole thing in just two weeks, as she always did – another positive sign.

Bette and Kathryn flew to New York first, before heading to England. B.D. drove from her farm in Pennsylvania to meet them in the city and say good-bye. Bette was happy to see her daughter but also puzzled that she would drive all that way since she had visited only once during the entire time she was recovering in New York. When they said goodbye, something seemed odd. Bette shook it off, too busy with her film to worry about it.

When she arrived in London, Bette was surprised by how good she felt. All that beach walking, climbing stairs, and swimming had gotten her into shape. Even the inevitable battles she fought during the shoot – when her costumes weren't ready, her favorite hairstylist Peggy Shannon wasn't there, the hotel wasn't right – were all promising indications that she was back to her usual form. And she was, remembering her lines and delivering a vintage performance.

"There is a 'perfect moment' for an actor, when you are at one with the words, the character and the action," Bette said later. "I realized how much I loved my profession. I had nearly forgotten how much, what a ham I was."

The high didn't last. From the ecstasy of performing – which she called her "return to the world of the living" – Bette was suddenly brought low by a stunning piece of news: Two days before *Murder with Mirrors* wrapped, Bette was told by her agent, Robbie Lantz, and her attorney, Harold Schiff, that B.D. had written a tell-all book called *My Mother's Keeper.*

They had not read the manuscript – it was scheduled for publication in the spring – but understood that it was a brutal indictment of Bette. Indeed, when the book was finally published,

*People* magazine described it as a "portrait of Davis as a mean-spirited, wildly neurotic, profane and pugnacious boozer who took out her anger at the world by abusing those close to her."

Shocked and deeply upset, Bette responded with a series of irate phone calls and letters to B.D., asking for an explanation, and demanding to see the manuscript before publication, which her daughter refused. "It was impossible for me to believe," Bette said later, that such a book could come from "my beloved B.D., whom sometimes I loved over and beyond my love of my work."

When *My Mother's Keeper* was finally published in May 1985 – just in time for Mother's Day – it was as searing as reported. B.D. portrayed her mother as a self-centered, emotionally abusive alcoholic. By 1973, she was often drunk by 10:00 a.m., B.D. wrote. "Happy?" she quotes her mother as saying. "Happy? I've never been happy . . . all my life I've had to fight the world. Everyone has always tried to get me."

B.D., now thirty-eight years old, also blamed her mother for not protecting her against her stepfather Gary Merrill, who would hit Bette and then B.D. and yell, "Get away from me and mind your own business, you little slut, or I'll give you the same as your mother!" Bette's response, B.D. claimed, was to scream at the child for making the situation worse.

In an interview with *People*, Merrill said, "There are kernels of truth in it but multiplied. Bette and I were both big drinkers, and sure I slapped her and B.D. We had physical fights, but not much more than the average family. Usually Bette pushed me first or something. I'm a lazy slob. I wouldn't start a fight."

There was much more, of course. B.D. wrote that Bette would sometimes threaten to kill herself in front of the kids. "Neither of you cares a damn about me," B.D. reported her mother said. "Well, we'll just see how you feel about it after I'm gone." At the time, B.D. was eight and Michael was three.

Bette's other parenting techniques, as explained by B.D., were also bizarre. When B.D. began dating as a teenager, she said, her mother urged her to be sexually active to avoid her own mistake of waiting until marriage to lose her virginity. At age fifteen, B.D. had a date with the twenty-three-year-old actor George Hamilton, already well-known from the 1960 film *Where the Boys Are*. "Well? Did he lay you?" Bette demanded when her daughter got home. When B.D. refused to answer, her mother snapped, "Well, he better have."

B.D. also claimed Bette would often lose her temper with Margot and call her "stupid" and "moron." "She spanked her constantly for everything," B.D. wrote. "She thought Margot should be treated with normal discipline."

Bette was also abusive to her grandchildren, Justin and Ashley, B.D. said. "She only hit him [Justin] three times," B.D. wrote, "but I know it was as hard as she could. The expression on her face was vicious. Justin screamed at the top of his lungs . . ." She also once put the boy in a dark room when he was four years old, saying "he better damn well stay in there and not try to come out till he'd learned his lesson."

While many compared *My Mother's Keeper* to the 1978 bestseller *Mommie Dearest* by Christina Crawford, daughter of Bette's nemesis Joan Crawford, there were some important differences. While *Mommie Dearest* was published after Joan Crawford's death, *My Mother's Keeper* came out while Bette was still alive, elderly, and recovering from her serious health problems. This generated considerable sympathy for Bette.

The timing of the book was shocking to those close to Bette. After all, her relationship with B.D. had seemed fine in recent years. About a year earlier, in January of 1984, Bette had thrown a glitzy twentieth-anniversary party for B.D. and Jeremy, who brought their two children for a ten-day visit with Bette at her home in Los Angeles. The gala event, at La Scala in Beverly Hills, was attended by stars such as Robert Wagner and Rock Hudson, who had known B.D. since she was a child.

Bette had also helped them out financially. She

had installed a pool at their Pennsylvania farm, for which B.D. and Jeremy were extremely grateful. By then, Jeremy had moved from film producing to the hay-trucking business. In February of 1983 – about two years before the book came out – he began having severe financial problems when the trucker's union went on strike. Bette came to the rescue with money that saved them from having to sell their beloved thirty-eight-acre farm and home.

Jeremy, who always had a difficult relationship with his mother-in-law, sent her a gushing thank-you note: "Your immense generosity in coming to our aid at a time of such importance to us is enormously appreciated," he said. "You saved the day for our business and did wonders for our personal morale."

B.D. was also thankful, writing to her mother, "I will never not be indebted to you for helping us through this frightening time and saving our home. I sincerely hope that our boys will look back at their childhoods in Pennsylvania as fondly as I do my childhood in Maine, and that it will stand them in good stead with a basis of good and real values as it did Mike and I. I love you very much."

So why did B.D. and Jeremy, who was B.D.'s unofficial editor, turn on Bette?

This much is known: B.D. decided to write the

memoir after that single visit with her mother in New York in September 1983, as Bette was recuperating from her surgery and stroke. But B.D. hesitated to publish – she had gathered too much explosive material about her mom, and it gave her pause. After all, for all her faults, Bette was still her mother. B.D. loved her and could plainly see that she was struggling with her long, drawn-out recovery.

But B.D. and Jeremy's lives changed in a big way in January 1984 – just weeks after their extravagant anniversary party in Los Angeles – when a man came to their door selling coupons for the local chamber of commerce. He was a born-again Christian who talked about his evangelical faith, Pentecostalism, and the power of the Holy Spirit. Until then, both B.D. and Jeremy were agnostics. But they were deeply taken by the man's message – Pentacostalism includes speaking in tongues and divine healing – and they experienced a full-out religious conversion. Soon they began raising their children, seven-year-old Justin, and fourteen-year-old Ashley, according to the teachings of their new faith.

By the fall of 1984 – around the time she visited her mother in New York as Bette was heading to London to film *Murder with Mirrors* – B.D. had decided to publish her book. She sold it to the publisher William Morrow for a $100,000 advance. The following year, as she went on her book-promotion tour, B.D. addressed the question everyone wanted to know: Why? "After I found the Lord, I realized there was a chance of a miracle in the literal sense with Mother," B.D. told *People*. "For Mother to change, she has to discover God through facing herself in this book. I want her to go to heaven."

In the epilogue of her book, B.D. made a final plea to her mom: "Regard this, Mother, as my cry in the wilderness, to prepare the way and make straight your path." Later, she said neither she nor Jeremy could recall actually writing that passage. "Some people have a ghostwriter," she said. "We have a Holy Ghost writer."

For some, those answers were not satisfying. If she only wanted to reach her mother, why didn't she just send her the manuscript rather than publish it? "She wouldn't have read it," B.D. told *People*. "She won't listen to anything she doesn't want to hear. She hangs up the phone or walks out the door. So I went the only route I felt would reach her: the public forum. What is seen by the world is the most important thing to Mother. This is essentially a public letter to my mother."

When the book came out, many of Bette's friends – and her son Michael – defended her, saying Bette did not abuse her daughter but did spoil her. The events described in the book, they said, were either exaggerated or taken out of context. Letters of support flowed in from Burt Reynolds, Meryl Streep, Mia Farrow, Sally Field, and others. CBS rebroadcast a *60 Minutes*' interview Mike Wallace did with B.D. in 1980 in which she praised Bette's skills as a mother and said she used many of her mom's rules in raising her own children.

And Merrill, despite his own tortured relationship with Bette, denied many of the book's allegations about her, telling CNN that B.D. was motivated by "cruelty and greed" and was trying to cash in on her mother's fame. (B.D. responded that a good portion of the book's profits would be going to her church.)

Michael Merrill, meanwhile, ended all contact with his sister. He called the book "a slap in the face to the whole family. Because it wasn't just mother. It was to all of us. That's the way I felt. Because now we were all going to have to deal with it. It was just a super-selfish thing to do. And it was going to put a cloud on Mother forever. It put a cloud on all of us forever."

Bette seized the chance to respond to her daughter in her own book, *This 'N That*, her second memoir, published in 1987 after many fits and starts. It had been mostly written when *My Mother's Keeper* came out two years earlier, Bette said, adding that she didn't change any of the passages that discussed her daughter. She did, however, add a letter to B.D., whom she addressed not by her first name, but by her last name.

> Dear Hyman,
>
> You ended your book with a letter to me. I have decided to do the same.
>
> There is no doubt you have a great potential as a writer of fiction. You have always been a great storyteller. I have often, lo these many years, said to you, "B.D., that is not the way it was. You are imagining things."
>
> Many of the scenes in your book I have played on the screen. It could be you have confused the "me" on the screen with the "me" who is your mother.

After objecting to what she said were false assertions that she has criticized some of her famous fellow actors, Bette went on:

> You constantly inform people that you wrote this book to help me understand you and your way of life better. Your goal was not reached. I am now utterly confused as to who you are or what your way of life is.
>
> The sum total of your having written this book is a glaring lack of loyalty and thanks for the very privileged life I feel you have been given.

Bette signed her name "Ruth Elizabeth" and ended the letter with a postscript:

> I hope someday I will understand the title *My Mother's Keeper*. If it refers to money, if my memory serves me right, I've been your keeper all these many years. I am continuing to do so, as my name has made your book about me a success.

After publication of her book, B.D. and her family moved to the city of Freeport on the Grand Bahama Island in the Caribbean. (She wrote a second book, *Narrow Is the Way* (1987) that also had harsh words about her mother but did not get nearly as much attention. Today, B.D. is pastor of her church in Charlottesville, Virginia and the author of three other books, all published by her ministry, including 2002's *The Rapture, The Tribulation and Beyond*, which contends, among other things, that in the U.S., babies are sacrificed on Halloween.)

As Bette was reeling from the trauma of B.D.'s betrayal, she accepted a role in her final television film, *As Summers Die*, shown on HBO in May of 1986. She appeared with Jamie Lee Curtis, already a star from the film *Trading Places* three years earlier, who said she took the part primarily for the chance to work with Bette, whom she admired greatly.

Bette's last truly memorable performance came soon afterward, when she co-starred with another legend, ninety-three-year-old Lillian Gish, in *The Whales of August*. Based on the play of the same name by David Berry, it tells the story of two elderly, widowed sisters near the end of their lives, spending a summer in a seaside house. It was filmed on Cliff Island, off the coast of Maine, not far from Ogunquit, where Bette had spent summers as a teenager.

The film gave Bette and Gish an opportunity to showcase their timeless talent and tell a poignant story of old age. In one scene, Bette's character, Libby, is frail and lying on a bed with the sun pouring into the room, highlighting her tiny frame. She gets up to find a box of keepsakes and puts a lock of dark hair to her face. It's as tender a scene as any Bette had ever filmed, overflowing with feeling, as she'd accomplished so many times before. As slight as she was, Bette could still create a wallop of emotion on the screen.

Of course, there were the usual conflicts on the set. Now seventy-eight and co-starring with an actress fifteen years her senior, Bette still wanted to dominate. She demanded – and received – top billing, which mortified Gish. ("Oh dear, I just can't deal with that sort of thing," she told *People* magazine later. "I don't care what they do with my name. If they leave it off, so much the better. It's the work I love, not the glory.")

During the filming, Bette rarely spoke to Gish or even looked at her, except when the script required it. Later, Gish seemed to take the high road – or perhaps was launching subtle digs – when she cried, “That face! Have you ever seen such a tragic face? Poor woman! How she must be suffering!”

Gish, after all her years in theater and film, was no innocent, however. When the cameras rolled, she pretended to have trouble hearing what Bette was saying – and Bette bought it. “She couldn’t have heard the cues if I’d shouted them through a bullhorn,” Bette said. Gish later confessed she was faking her hearing loss to drive Bette crazy. It worked. As they re-shot each scene, with director Lindsay Anderson shouting out the lines to Gish, Bette seethed.

*The Whales of August* earned mixed-to-positive reviews when it came out in October of 1987, with *People* singling Bette out for praise: “Bette crawls across the screen like a testy old hornet on a windowpane, snarling, staggering, twitching - a symphony of misfired synapses.”

The last film Bette ever made, the comedy *Wicked Stepmother*, came about when the horror film director Larry Cohen saw her presenting a Golden Globe award in 1986 and wanted to help her out. Still recovering from her stroke, Bette limped onto the stage, her body emaciated, her face still partially paralyzed. “It was a shocking sight to behold,” Cohen said later.

Knowing Bette loved nothing more than to work, Cohen thought he would honor her by creating a role just for her: a chain-smoking witch who marries a widower, wreaks havoc on his daughter's family, and insists on being called "mom." Flattered, Bette accepted. But after meeting the star, Cohen's agent, Peter Sabiston, was incredulous. "How can you even consider making a movie with a woman in her condition?" he said.

Realizing the risks, Cohen plowed ahead, bewitched by Bette's charm and the idea of directing the great star. As production neared, he got calls from her at all hours of the day and night. In her raspy voice, she would say things like, "Larry, I've decided that my character must have red hair rather than my normal color." Then she would hang up, without even a goodbye. On the set, she smoked 100 Vantage cigarettes every day, with Kathryn following her around to make sure she was never without one.

But after just one week of shooting, Bette abruptly quit. Cohen scrambled to finish the film, rewriting his script to explain why Bette's character suddenly disappears (her spirit inhabits the body of a cat). Meanwhile, Bette's attorney and longtime manager, Harold Schiff, claimed that she quit because she had been mistreated, didn't like the script, was poorly directed by Cohen, and was subject to hazardous working conditions.

As it turns out, that was all a cover. In June of 1988,

Bette had to testify under oath at a legal deposition so the insurance company could determine fault for the delay in filming. There, she admitted that weeks before production, her bridgework cracked. Bette said nothing to Cohen and tried to get by but failed. "She could barely get the lines out because of the necessary pauses to readjust the bridge with her tongue," Cohen said later. "For a perfectionist like Bette, this was pure hell."

According to Cohen, Bette did not let on about her condition because she was worried that other studios would refuse to hire her. Actors – especially older ones – who quit for medical reasons are often considered uninsurable. Even at age eighty, her body ravaged by age and infirmity, that's how badly she still wanted to work.

After *Wicked Stepmother*, Bette hit the rounds on the talk-show circuit, being interviewed by Johnny Carson, Joan Rivers, Larry King, and David Letterman. She freely discussed her long career and failed marriages but refused to discuss her daughter B.D. And the honors continued to roll in: the Kennedy Center Honor, the Legion of Honor from France, the Campione d'Italia and the Film Society of Lincoln Center's Lifetime Achievement Award.

What few people knew, however, is that her cancer had returned. It first became evident in January of 1989, when she was being feted at the Sixth Annual American Cinema Awards in Beverly Hills. Soon after she sat down, Bette was taking a bite of her salad when she slumped forward, her face landing in her salad plate.

An ambulance was called. Fearing that she was dead, someone gave her mouth-to-mouth resuscitation. Immediately, Bette roared back to life. When the actor Glenn Ford leaned down to talk to her, she looked up and seemed to recall the bad blood between them during the filming of *Pocketful of Miracles* in 1961, more than a quarter-century earlier. "Get him out of here!" she cried.

A few moments later, she was in fine form, irascible as ever. "Come on, I'm not dying," she said. "I'm going to get my award." And she did, giving a long speech that convinced some in the audience that she would live forever.

But Bette's days on earth were winding down. Her final performance was not a film, nor a stage play, nor a television appearance. It was a trip to Spain, to the San Sebastian film festival, where she was scheduled to receive the festival's prestigious Donostia Award in September of 1989. There, she played perhaps her greatest role: Bette Davis, Famously Bitchy Film Icon.

It was a long, grueling trip, from Los Angeles to New York to Paris to Biarritz, France, and finally to San Sebastian. During the festival, Bette spent five days at the luxurious Hotel Maria

Cristina throwing her usual tantrums. She had demanded that her cab driver from the airport speak English; when he did not, a bewildered bystander was pressed into service. She brought somewhere between thirty and fifty suitcases, and when several went missing, she exploded. She dismissed her makeup artist for being too young, causing her terrified replacement to rush to make herself look older.

Getting around in a wheelchair, Bette refused to allow herself to be photographed in it – much like her hero, Franklin Delano Roosevelt. She banned photographers from her press conference, where she wowed the crowd with her wisecracks and spoke candidly about her disastrous marriages. She wore a wig and used makeup to approximate eyebrows. Through it all, she remained as sharp as ever. In her acceptance speech, she cracked, "If they'd waited any longer to give me this award, I wouldn't be here to receive it."

Despite her unrepentant diva attitude – or perhaps because of it – Bette was showered with praise and adulation from the festival organizers and fans. Her magnetic presence was one of the greatest moments in the event's history. "Miss Davis," festival director Diego Galan told her in her final stage appearance, "We all love you."

When the festival ended, Bette was too weak to make the long journey back to the United States.

So she and Sermak flew to Paris, where she was admitted to the American Hospital in the suburb of Neuilly-sur-Seine.

After examining her, the hospital physicians told Sermak that Bette did not have long to live. Then they explained the situation to Bette, who thanked them. Bette immediately began listing all the things she wanted Sermak to do - sign checks, cancel a dinner date, and contact her friend and attorney Harold Schiff to tell him that she would not be getting out of this particular mess alive.

On October 6, 1989, at 11:20 pm – less than forty-eight hours after arriving in Paris – Bette Davis died. The cause of death was metastasized breast cancer. She was eighty-one years old.

Bette Davis was gone but hardly forgotten. The volcanic way she lived her life ensured that. Even in death, she wanted the world to pay attention. “I don’t want anyone sending money to any little charity instead of flowers,” she once said with typical bluntness. “I want millions of flowers . . . I want everyone to weep. Copiously.”

# EPILOGUE

## "THERE'S BETTE DAVIS. THEN THERE'S EVERYBODY ELSE."

Bette was buried on October 12, 1989, in a family crypt at Forest Lawn Memorial Park in the Hollywood Hills overlooking the Warner Brothers studio where she spent so much of her career.

Alongside her in the Davis crypt is her mother Ruthie and her sister, Bobby. As always, Bette gets top billing, with her name in larger type, above the words, "She did it the hard way."

On November 2, more than 350 actors, writers, directors, and producers attended a memorial service on Warner Brothers Stage 18. It was fitting that Bette, who lived to work, was honored on a movie set that was not elaborately redecorated for the occasion – but spare and ready for the next film. The klieg lights, booms, and camera dollies seemed to be waiting for some director to jump out of her seat, set up the lights, and cry, "Action!"

"Somewhere in heaven, there's someone saying, 'buckle your seat belts, it's going to be a bumpy eternity,'" the actor James Woods said in his tribute. Friends such as Robert Wagner, Roddy McDowell, and Stephanie Powers were there, as was Bette's assistant Kathryn Sermak and singer Kim Carnes of "Bette Davis Eyes" fame. Bette's estranged daughter B.D. did not attend.

"Thank God she worked as hard as she did," said Angela Lansbury in an emotional eulogy. "It was bravura acting of the first order, and all of us gained by it." President George H.W. Bush sent a telegram that said, "Although she was a self-described terror, all America loved her and we loved her."

In her ten-page will, dated September 2, 1987, Bette clearly stated that she was intentionally leaving out several family members – B.D. and her two children, Ashley and Justin, as well as Bette's disabled daughter Margot – without explanation. Her estate, valued at between $600,000 and $1 million, was split equally between her son Michael Merrill and her loyal assistant, Kathryn Sermak.

Bette's exclusion of Margot from her will may have been a final dig at Merrill, who – ever since their dispute in the late sixties about where their daughter should live – had been paying for her care at Lochland. Merrill would pay those bills until his death in 1990 and had set up a trust, managed by his son Michael, that continued to provide for Margot. (In 2008's *Dark Victory: The Life of Bette Davis*, author Ed Sikov reported Margot was still at Lochland.)

As might be expected, Bette's loyalty to Sermak caused friction with some of her closest friends, who questioned the young woman's intentions. Chuck Pollack, a friend for fifteen years, said Bette had become distant after hiring Sermak, who drove her other friends away with a goal of making Bette rely on her only. Intentional or not, Sermak became the person Bette felt she could depend on most in her later years and rewarded her amply for it.

Bette also scattered some of her most prized possessions among friends and family. She gave clothing to Michael's wife Chou Chou. Her old friend Robin Brown was given a painting and a sapphire watch. Bobby's daughter, Fay Forbes, was left six silver condiment holders that Bette had received from Ruthie.

Sermak received some jewelry, furniture, cookbooks, and other items, including Bette's two Oscars. She later sold the statuette for *Dangerous* to the Planet Hollywood restaurant chain – though in 2002, director Steven Spielberg acquired it at an auction for $180,000 and donated it to the Academy of Motion Picture Arts and Sciences. Spielberg also bought Bette's Jezebel Oscar for $578,000 and donated it to the Academy as well. Proceeds from the sale went to the Bette Davis Foundation for young actors, established in 1997 by Sermak and Michael Merrill.

Spielberg apparently recognized these Oscar trophies for what they were: mementos from a woman who blazed her way into the new world of talkies in the 1930s and for more than a half century left an indelible mark on the minds of moviegoers and moviemakers alike. Among Bette's many honors were two Academy Awards, ten Oscar nominations, one Emmy, and countless other awards that poured in from countries around the globe.

Even in death, her star continued to rise. In 1999, Bette was ranked behind only Katharine Hepburn among actresses in the American Film Institute's movie-industry poll of the "50 Greatest American Screen Legends." In 2006, her masterful portrayal of Margo Channing in *All About Eve* ranked fifth on *Premiere* magazine's list of "100 Greatest Performances of All Time."

Bette's impact on other actors was overpowering. "Bette Davis was the greatest single actor of either sex in the history of cinema, bar none," actor James Woods once said. "There's Bette Davis. Then there's everybody else."

Women in film, in particular, credited her with opening vistas they never imagined possible. "Bette Davis was my heroine as a child," said Gena Rowlands, who co-starred with her in *Strangers: The Story of a Mother and Daughter*. "I was shocked by her. Because, when I was young, all the actresses played sweetie pies and nice girls. And then there was Bette."

Jane Fonda agreed. "Just watching Bette Davis on the screen was empowering to women," she said. "It was like, 'This is what's possible.' This is the range and depth that is possible for a woman. Enough already with these one-dimensional women. She expanded our range of possibilities."

When the cameras were not rolling, Bette was always brutally, honestly herself – which, of course, wreaked havoc on her personal life. But in a Hollywood landscape full of fakery and superficiality, this slashing approach to life and work ultimately gained the deep respect of her peers. It was perhaps that honesty, barbed though it was, that most endeared her to people – even those she enraged, making her an unforgettable presence in their lives.

Bette Davis was more than just a survivor. In a life that was messy, painful, terribly lonely, and often chaotic, she thrived. "Indestructible," she once said. "That's the word that's often used to describe me. I suppose it means that I just overcame everything."

# SOURCES

Val Adams, "Bette Davis Signs for TV Series," *The New York Times, September 3, 1964.*

*Charles Affron, Star Acting (New York, New York: Dutton, 1977).*

*Eugene Archer, "Fasten Your Seatbelts - Here's Bette Davis," The New York Times, March 7, 1965.*

*Mary Astor, My Story (New York, New York: Doubleday, 1959).*

*Brooks Atkinson, "Case of Bette Davis," The New York Times, December 21, 1952.*

*Jeanne Basinger, "The Real Margo Channing's Fasten-Your-Seatbelts Life," The New York Times, November 12, 2007.*

*Sally Bedell, "Bette Davis Joins ABC's Fall Lineup," The New York Times, May 5, 1983.*

*A. Scott Berg, Goldwyn (New York, New York: Knopf, 1989).*

*Thomas F. Brady, "Bette Davis Seeks to Leave Warners," The New York Times, July 26, 1949.*

*Thomas F. Brady, "Bette Davis Star of 'Ethan Frome,'" The New York Times, February 7, 1948.*

*Vincent Canby, "Bette Davis: The Moral, The Myth," The New York Times, October 15, 1989.*

*Gary Carey, More About All About Eve (New York, New York: Random House, 1972).*

*Charlotte Chandler, The Girl Who Walked Home Alone: Bette Davis, a Personal Biography (New York, New York: Simon & Schuster, 1983).*

*Douglas W. Churchill, "Warner Buys 'The Corn Is Green' for Bette Davis," The New York Times, April 2, 1941.*

*Joan Collins, Past Imperfect (New York, New York: Simon & Schuster, 1984).*

*Shaun Considine, Bette and Joan: The Divine Feud (New York, New York: Dutton, 1989).*

*Richard Corliss, "She Did It the Hard Way," Time, October 16, 1989.*

*Glenn Collins, "Bette Davis Is Saluted, Spirit and Acid*

*Wit Intact," The New York Times, April 25, 1989.*

*Glenn Collins, "Tribute for a Dauntless Bette Davis," The New York Times, April 20, 1989.*

*John Culhane, "Bette Davis: 'You Must Care, Everything Has to Be Right,'" The New York Times, April 13, 1980.*

*Bette Davis, "Movies Vs. Broadway: Bette Davis Champions Movies," The Christian Science Monitor, April 24, 1989.*

*Bette Davis, This 'N That (New York, New York: Putnam's, 1987).*

*Bette Davis, This Lonely Life (New York, New York: Putnam's, 1961).*

*Bette Davis and Bill Davidson, "All About Me," Collier's, November 25 and December 9, 1955.*

*Bette Davis, "Uncertain Glory," Ladies home Journal, July 1941.*

*Neal Gabler, An Empire of Their Own (New York, New York: Crown, 1988).*

*Lawrence Grobel, The Hustons (New York, New York: Scribner's, 1989).*

*Mel Gussow, "Bette Davis: One of the First to Look Like 'a Real Person,'" The New York Times, January 19, 1977.*

*Gladys Hall, "Bette Davis Life Story," Modern*

*Screen, March 1941.*

*Joshua Hammer, "Fade-Out of a Feisty Legend," Newsweek, October 16, 1989.*

*Helen Hayes, My Life in Three Acts (New York, New York: Touchstone, 1990).*

*Charles Higham, Bette (New York, New York: Macmillan, 1981).*

*Clive Hirschhorn, The Warner Brothers Story (New York, New York: Crown, 1979).*

*Wayne Hogan, "Thanks, Bette, For This One," The Christian Science Monitor, November 24, 1989.*

*Hedda Hopper with James Brough, The Whole Truth and Nothing But (New York, New York: Doubleday, 1963).*

*B. D. Hyman and Jeremy Hyman, Narrow Is the Way (New York, New York: Morrow, 1987).*

*B. D. Hyman, My Mother's Keeper (New York, New York: Morrow, 1985).*

*Walter Kerr, "Bette Davis - Winner and Still Champ," The New York Times, March 20, 1977.*

*Albin Krebs, "Bette Davis, A Queen of Hollywood, Dies at 81," The New York Times, October 8, 1989.*

*Barbara Leaming, Bette Davis: A Biography (New York, New York: Summit, 1992).*

*Sonia Lee, "The Untold Bette," Screenplay, November 1935.*

*Robert Lindsey, "Film Institute Honors Bette Davis," The New York Times, March 3, 1977.*

*Joshua Logan, Movie Stars, Real People, and Me (New York, New York: Delacorte, 1978).*

*Axel Madsen, William Wyler (New York, New York: Crowell, 1973).*

*Arthur Marx, Goldwyn (New York, New York: Norton, 1976).*

*Janet Maslin, "TV: Bette Davis as Elderly 'Mrs. Cimino,'" The New York Times, February 3, 1982.*

*Cathleen McGuigan, "Mommie, Joanie, and Baby B.D.," Newsweek, March 30, 1987.*

*John T. McManus, "Bette Davis Here," The New York Times, March 29, 1936.*

*Gary Merrill, Bette, Rita, and the Rest of My Life (New York, New York: Yankee, 1988).*

*Roy Moseley, Better Davis: An Intimate Memoir (New York, New York: Donald I. Fine, 1990).*

*Elliot Norton, "A Star Is Educated," The New York Times, November 30, 1952.*

*Frank S. Nugent, "Bette Davis Returns to Strand in 'Marked Woman,'" The New York Times, April 12, 1937.*

*Lawrence J. Quirk, Fasten Your Seatbelts: The Passionate Life of Bette Davis (New York, New York: Morrow, 1990).*

*Terrence Rafferty, "The Bold and the Bad and the Bumpy Nights," The New York Times, March 30, 2008.*

*Rex Reed, "Fasten Your Seatbelts," The New York Times, November 4, 2007.*

*Rex Reed, "'I Was Tougher Than Everybody Else,' Bette Davis," The New York Times, March 10, 1968.*

*David Richards, "The Bette Davis Who Came to Dinner," The New York Times, December 8, 1994.*

*Jeffrey Robinson, Better Davis (New York, New York: Proteus, 1982).*

*Tony Rogers, "Eye-Opening Collection on Bette Davis," Telegram & Gazette, April 9, 1990.*

*Alvin Sanoff, "What Ever Happened to Hollywood?" U.S. News & World Report, December 8, 1986.*

*Richard Schickel, "Bette," Film Comment, March 1989.*

*Murray Schumach, "Two Stars Discuss Hollywood Life," The New York Times, May 31, 1961.*

*Ed Sikov, Dark Victory: The Life of Bette Davis (New York, New York: Holt, 2007).*

*Scott S. Smith, "Davis Steered Her Straight Up in Hollywood Standout," Investor's Business Daily, November 1, 2013.*

*James Spada, More Than a Woman: An Intimate Biography of Bette Davis (New York, New York: Bantam, 1993).*

*David Sterritt, "Bette: Red-Hot Spark of Originality," The Christian Science Monitor, October 16, 1989.*

*Louise Sweeney, "Bette Davis: On the Heels of a New Honor and a New Film, a Screen Legend Looks Back Over Her Sixty-Year Career," The Christian Science Monitor, December 28, 1987.*

*Angela Taylor, "Bette Davis: 'I'm a Hausfrau at Heart,'" The New York Times, December 8, 1970.*

*Howard Thompson, "At Home With Bette Davis, West Coast Visitor and Maine Citizen, The New York Times, July 10, 1955.*

*Alexander Walker, Bette Davis (New York, New York: Weidenfeld & Nicolson, 1986).*

*Jack Warner, My First Hundred Years in Hollywood (New York, New York: Random House, 1965).*

*"Bette Davis and Marilyn Monroe - Were They Alike in Any Way?" Telegram & Gazette, May 8, 2014.*

*"Bette Davis and Errol Flynn Still Thrilling After All These Years," Telegram & Gazette, October 23, 2013.*

*"1934 Star Turn: Bette Davis, Of Human Bondage," Newsweek, September 1998.*

*"First Encounters: Joan Crawford and Bette Davis,"*

*The Atlantic, September 1991.*

*"Bette Davis Honored in Paris," The New York Times, February 24, 1986.*

*"Bette Davis Bars Return to 'Hotel,'" The New York Times, February 7, 1984.*

*"Bette Davis Suffering With Two Broken Ribs," The New York Times, March 12, 1979.*

*"Bette Davis Wins Delay," The New York Times, June 17, 1964.*

*"Bette Davis Signed for 'Empty Canvas,'" The New York Times, April 18, 1963.*

*"Bette Davis Takes Ad; Seeks Job, Won't Travel," The New York Times, September 22, 1962.*

*"Bette Davis Sues," The New York Times, October 5, 1961.*

*"Bette Davis Divorced," The New York Times, July 7, 1960.*

*"Bette Davis Seeks Divorce," The New York Times, May 4, 1960.*

*"Bette Davis Seeks Separation," The New York Times, June 11, 1957.*

*"Bette Davis Sued for Alimony, The New York Times, November 2, 1954.*

*"Bette Davis's Jaw Operated On," The New York*

*Times, March 17, 1953.*

*"Bette Davis Collapses," The New York Times, October 20, 1952.*

*"Bette Davis to Resume Role," The New York Times, October 23, 1952.*

*"Bette Davis Married," The New York Times, July 29, 1950.*

*"Bette Davis Gets Divorce," The New York Times, July 4, 1950.*

*"Bette Davis Gets Child Custody," The New York Times, June 8, 1950.*

*"Bette Davis Is Married," The New York Times, December 1, 1945.*

*"Bette Davis to Wed on Coast Tomorrow," The New York Times, November 29, 1945.*

*"Bette Davis's Salary Tops," The New York Times, March 14, 1945.*

*"Bette Davis Denies Romance," The New York Times, September 28, 1944.*

*"Bette Davis Heads Canteen Again," The New York Times, April 19, 1944.*

*"Bette Davis's Husband Dies From a Fall," The New York Times, August 26, 1943.*

*"Bette Davis Heads Group," The New York Times,*

*November 8, 1941.*

*"Dog Bites Bette Davis," The New York Times, September 14, 1941.*

*"Acts to Divorce Bette Davis," The New York Times, November 23, 1938.*

*"Bette Davis Suspended by Warners for Refusing Role," The New York Times, April 2, 1938.*

*"Bette Davis Barred from British Film," The New York Times, October 20, 1936.*

*"Bette Davis Held 'Naughty,'" The New York Times, October 15, 1936.*

*"H. O. Nelson Jr. Weds Bette Davis," The New York Times, August 20, 1932.*

new
Word
city

Made in the USA
Monee, IL
26 October 2020

46130556R00216